How to Love

By Hitachi Choparazzi

Acknowledgements

I'd like to give all due praise to the Creator of the universe and life itself. My kids Jr., Pierre, Kylan, and daughter China. G-Ma Lawson, Mama Lisa, my sisters and aunties who help give me a point of view and perspective on love and how to treat someone you truly loved. Most of all to the special woman that I made a spiritual and all-around love connection with. The matching missing great puzzle piece in my lifetime. I love you eternally. Our love is full of surprises and bliss.

ATTN:

This *How to Love* book is from the author's perspective of love, from a love analysis point of view.

This book is to show you how to love. Teaching you practices, elements, methods, and principles of love. Effective love solutions and show you how to discover your true loveprint from your heart. To be subjectable for love and a potential matchmate and lifetime partner.

However, this book is not to give you an instant gratification of love and to meet your soulmate, or guarantee you get swept off your feet with a magical broom, or to find love and marriage.

This book is only meant to add value to you, teach you how to love, awareness, consciousness, building structure on principles and core beliefs for a loving foundation without self-doubt. To open up love topics and dialogues. As a resource to make love better. To give the reader that seeks love realization on how to find their own loveprint and identity stored deep inside of them versus someone else's or the world's love reassurance. To educate, elevate, and inspire people how to love and find true love within. A therapeutic read.

Contents

Foreword

I see more reality dating and finding love shows or showmances. Nowadays they all just have the recipe for ratings vs. true injgredients for love. Love isn't just finding a connection live, or in front of a T.V. audience of millions for clout, or social media likes. There is no way to tell if the person is being authentic. Is that their true individuality off camera, or a T.V. public persona masked?

Everyone is on dating apps in this new tech era looking for love in all the wrong places. You must know, identify, and learn your own unique loveprint. Also, what is your checklist or prerequisite for true love and subjectable matchmate?

If your roots are not planted deeply, your relationship will blow away and your love will dissolve. It's inevitable break-ups, love loss, and the pure illusion of love.

Everyone is seeking true romance and interested in creating their own love story and getting swept off their feet with a magical broom, directly or indirectly. To be appreciated and loved, validation from others. Love isn't being lucky. It's more being aligned with chemistry and a love periodic table. It takes real love to evolve with your heart rhythm. A true connection.

Relationships are so important and to open up dialogue to further your partnership/friendship and perpetuate your love. It's good to engage in being a better person and partner. Being open with communication that strips the fear of anxiety, nervous, or avoidance patterns, which can lead to natural drawn negativity, fears, failures, and judgements of distrust.

We develop a template of what love means from our parents, siblings, and peers, which is wrong and not our realistic loveprint design of your heart. We become in our relationship habits and patterns the same as our parents and social norms showed us. The unconscious comes and projects your subconscious. Then we look for the same familiar patterns again and again. Inflicting each partner and person with the same imagery as the last. Thinking love will happen when it does like your fairy tale projects.

I will show you how to become more conscious of love, find your inner unique loveprint, and your ideal matchmate. It's a step-by-step, day-by-day practice model to take effect of the impulsive form of love imagery projected in you that's being used against your building blocks foundation of love biochemistry, hindering and restricting you from lifetime love.

You will reverse and retrain your love psyche. Then be compatible, open to your potential matchmate. Romance and companionship make best loving lasting relationships from various concoctions of love, including love ingredients, elements, and principles of love.

You will be surprised of how many people don't know how to truly love and ranging from all age groups. Therefore, you are not alone. Plus, it is evident in divorce rates, shattered families, and high break-up ratios. People are so disconnected and out of whack from their true loveprint essence.

I'll show you how to reconnect and rewire that broken or damaged wire from your head blockage back to your heart. To get your vibrant flow and heart radius back in sync with your loveprint, finally.

By you taking the time out to read this book and the initiative of love shows you're already on the path to discovery of your loveprint, too. You have to know how to love and adore yourself, way before you can successfully love someone else. You don't want to be like so many other people of the world and waste somebody else's or your time. Life is meant for love and growth. We only have a certain amount of time to find love on our timeline of life, which causes so many people the dire mistake of trying to rush love or attempting to force love before their prime time expires in their love psyche and life.

This book will show you how to love, or someone else how to potentially love you, too.

- Chapter 1 -

"Inception"

Inception is the beginning, where it all started. The origin of imagery of love that was placed into your head either by sound, visual, or someone else's ideology of love. We pick it up indirectly and don't realize we have actually retained someone else's lovebug theorem, derailing from your true divine path to your loveprint, which alters your senses, mindframe, and triggers blockage, leading up to emotional and physical barriers, furthering you from your inceptional dream lover. It's hard to overcome and an aspect that most people are not aware of.

Usually this issue leads to patterns of behaviors. Bad habits and choices. Binge eating, emotional distress, unhealthy fatigue, and very indecisive. This impairs your judgement and puts your subconscious further into autopilot, projecting images like a dream. With all this distortion through your brainwaves of rhythmic fluctuations voltage, you cannot signal a current produced by your brainwaves to your heart, further jeopardizing your loveprint.

All of us are entitled to our own love cues, cravings of intimacy, and the anthropology of love.

Inception of love is where you identify love from the early stages of your life. As a child you pick up details of love, illicit habit-forming all from your parents, such as dysfunctional household and become dysfunctional norms in you as an adult, too. You absorb human behavior and human closeness as a kid easily influenced. You are not yet aware of senses of reality. Instead you pick up traits and characteristics from your parents' journey of sunken love, and you carry it into adulthood to fill out. Your parents' love life has an effect on you indirectly or directly since day one.

Some parents don't get divorced and stay together because of the kids' sake. However, the disconnect that can't be fixed is unhealthy for the kids, too.

Now the child believes you can't trust love because of their perception of love. They often get neglected because their parents are going through suffering, hurt, and a negative cycled relationship.

They adopt what their parents went through and being divorced, negative environment, single parenting, and all reflect on the kids' inception process and become innate practice. It may lay dormant for years, then manifest and progress as lovelorn.

Kids need to see happy and healthy relationships. This is why most people have relationship issues stemming from their parents and childhood created the problems. This dysfunction isn't abnormal anymore. It's a huge problem and norm nowadays.

A half million break-ups from relationships occur every day. The divorce rate is 50 percent. The depression, anxiety rate is above average and induced a lot of prescription drugs. This all plays a huge factor from your inception of dysfunction, lack of true knowledge of love, and self-sabotage of relationships.

We not only gain weight in pounds, we also gain weight heavy on heart and stress of your mind. We cannot be strong and balanced if our mental health is out of alignment.

During this inception identity phase, we adopt a psychological template of love from our parents, peers, siblings, or public. This emotional effect could vary from pictures, words, and negative adversity visuals of love seen played out. This is what first triggers your love cues to play on repeat in your scripted subconscious like a movie. Then you play it out in reality, looking for that same familiar love scene of that favorite spot in your head versus the same spot and rhythm of your heart.

This is because you are living a lie and someone else's ideology and predominance of love, furthering disconnecting from yours. We must be predetermined to first recognize that it exists. We are humans of habits and naturally copy and repeat others since we were infants. The preconceived notion of environmental influences. Then we can recreate the psychological effect and install new software in your subconscious, upgrading it with new pictures and visual love cues of health and happiness. A reverse psychology and reverse engineering effect. It's not a biohack quick fix. This is a day-to-day, step-by-step process and approach to implement, which I will show you how to by reading this book and what to put into practice.

If you see your parents or single parent have a loving relationship, then more likely you will, too, adopting all the ways your parents loved and treated one another. Also picking up ways your parents view love, and an emotional response with them. It's not even from kids just being easily influenced by parents; it's them picking up perceptions of how they should love, too. We pick up survival skills and loving skills, too, when we're young, then store them into our memory banks and subconscious mind as well.

However, if your parents and household was toxic, fighting, arguing, and an all-around negative environment stemming from physical, mental, verbal, alcohol, and drug abuse, then you can also adapt the same characteristic. Some even mistake love for affection or attraction, which alter relationships and chances at finding true love. Not every connection is a love connection. A lot is misguided between lust versus love. Lust wears off and usually a sexual craving versus love is a perpetual feeling and strongest emotion on the planet, followed by the passion that drives and motivates us behind love. Sex is not better than love; it does play a contributing factor role in love.

Usually people's relationship problems occur from habits of inception process as a kid and same as their parents. If you also have problems with different partners, it's usually not short-term relationships, because you are looking for that same inceptional prototype of love bestowed inside you from childhood of your parents. Whereas, it's not your inner heart and loveprint, you are simply living someone else's. You don't ever sit and think to yourself that the love path you're seeking in your life is not reality and is actually someone else's that got imprinted on your psyche and set on repeat in your subconscious. How many of us actually unveil this or realize we suffer from this problem? With the distractions of the world and daily rituals, how can you distinguish this matter in your relationships? Especially now with the digital era, everyone has a 5-second attention span. A goldfish has a 6-second attention span. So how can we reciprocate this with our partners or a shrink who cannot go into our heads and fix for us beside prescribing meds as mood stabilizers?

We be hard on ourselves because we don't get the instant love and performance results we put out that we strive for and want back the same or tenfold with ulterior motives because of, again, our inceptional ideologies.

Most people believe the power of persuasion and passion to sway their partner or mold them in the liking of love design they desire. Your perspective is not aligned with your heart patterns nor the aspect of your partner's true heart. You must disengage all prior love status quos and norm arrangements seeking love voids. Awaken your senses and conscience to grasp and recognize it's time for a change and shift. Flip the switch in your head and ignite your heart's melody with your loveprint unanimously. However, the methodology I teach you will not be a simultaneous effect with instant result of love and all bad habits dropped. You cannot be single-minded in love or singularity approach for a quick love hack. True love takes time like fine wine and has a love periodic table of elements and structure.

It's a huge vastly gray area of love and people's inception and perception of love. How they see love and view love from life's perspective. It may be retained generational love practices or cliché prerequisites of love and foundation that's not pragmatic.

For example, if you ask someone, "What is love?" Some will say a noun because it's just an idea/thing. Whereas, most people would describe love as a defined verb, saying it's an action, which is also true. I definitely would define love as an action and verb more than a noun. Most people never took the time out to Google love. It's not because it's too taboo. People all have their own definition and assume the world views love as the same aspect through their peripheral spectrum.

Webster Dictionary defines...

Love, *noun*: 1) strong affection; 2) warm attachment; 3) attraction based on sexual desire; 4) a beloved person; 5) unselfish, loyal, and benevolent concern for others

2 Love, *verb*: 1) cherish; 2) to feel a passion, devotion, or tenderness for; 3) caress; 4) to take pleasure in

Therefore, it is so many aspects of love and elements. I will break down the different characteristics and challenge the cliché narratives of love. Like the Third Webster definition of love as a noun above as attraction based on sexual desire. Not making love, but actual love. Most of us view that as lust, not love. If that were the true cause, the whole world would have love, and know what love is, then finally know how to love as well. However, the second love defined as a verb hinted more of love's principles. I will simplify and further break down for you to grasp, evaluate, and execute your love path. Breaking through the blockage and discovering your true loveprint dynamic.

"You had a lot of crooks trying to steal your heart, but you never figured out how to love." —Lil Wayne

The rapper Lil Wayne made a melodic song over a decade ago delivering a strong message that he, too, recognized the problematic of people looking for love in all the wrong places. Whereas, people mistaking validation for love, not realizing it's actually self-validation or being validated by others they truly seek. They're not at fault, they just never understood or identified the problem and its origin. Where it came from, why it exists, and what all problems or dysfunction they suffer from their childhood and bring into relationships, constantly sabotaging them. That was adopted.

You can also be suffering from narcissism. Not by nature, but indirectly self-sabotaging that you picked up someone's narcissistic trait. A lot of independent people have this characteristic and self-centered and absorbed. They are not in denial about them possessing the trait, they simply don't have a clue or knowledge attributes they suffer from narcissism qualities.

We weren't meant to live by ourselves and to be alone. We are social humans by nature and have to communicate and socialize. If not in groups and crowds, then we still need someone to confide with. It's just simply the human in us.

Therefore, an individual that grew up being in an environment where they were taught or influenced to establish their independence early on, they do just that. They take it into their relationships and still be all about self versus partner or loved ones. It's out of pure habitualness. They are blinded to the detrimental effect they cause on people or partner in their relationships. Whether family, spouse, or friends, they still will blame the other party or recipient, unaware that they are reclusive and solely the cause and blame on the relationship shortcomings, blocks, and dire damage.

The solution to your initial inceptions that you picked up as a child and stuck into your psyche in your cortex playing on repeat on your subconscious, you must remove, redirect, reprogram, and detoxify. Then apply.

Just like the Matrix effect, all of our inceptions of love were programmed in us. We have to be aware by identifying our troubleshoot areas. Then, once evaluated, reprogram our subconscious by being conscious. Once you reform your mind to know the truth and discover the real you and real loveprint, your subconscious will pick it up, and you will start acting out on it with a new movie and love story played out by your own written and directed version, not scripted by someone else's. Start telling, thinking, and believing in yourself.

This method is an effective strategy you have to put into practice day by day. Your subconscious will create your reality. It will remove any toxin or ideology effects imprinted because it will tell you that is not real or your own loveprint. You don't have to be afraid to fall in love or fear loving someone wholeheartedly, giving them your all and everlasting efforts.

In this book, I will also teach you habits of good and bad, and the process to break them, too.

- Chapter 2 -

"Perception"

What is your love status? What is your perception of love? How about your perception of others? And your overall perception of life and love?

Perception is awareness of one's environment through physical sensation, and the ability to understand, insight, comprehension. This chapter of perception I will outline the awareness, and cause, and effect of perception, along with the imagery effect and influential norms.

People's perception is how they not only view and read things, it's also how they interpret, digest, and analyze things, too. Including love and circumstances from their everyday lives.

Imagery is key and plays a significant role because of how we see and perceive the world, solidify our state of mind between fiction and fact. Also our imagery of love imprint and impact evolves around our developed projectiles in a specific designed pattern or plan by perception.

It's two types of perceptional effects. One is your own personal perception. Then you have reciprocal perception, too, where you perceive as others or the world society views. That form of imagery is being impersonated and acted out upon.

For example, some people have a perception of security as love. They want to feel secure and well-established as love from their mate. Secure in financial status, not just well-being's sake. Just like a lot of celebrity couples want someone usually equally compensated in wealth versus being equally compatible or wealthy in spirit and health. Which is also why Hollywood divorces are at a 87 percent rate now. This applies for all people adjoining relationships just for the secure status.

Even though we develop these perceptions, it's not hereditary. It is recessive as far as characteristic of multitude, though. This also plays a big part in your subconsciousness. The conscience.

You must understand your subconscious versus your consciousness, and how your subconscious plays on your imagery and projects it in congruence.

Subconscious is the existing in the mind without entering conscious awareness, and the mental activities just below the threshold of consciousness.

Whereas, conscious is being aware, known or felt by one's inner self, mentally awake or alert. Not asleep or unconscious. Also, the upper level of mental life of which a person is aware and conscious.

You can basically look at it as your brain being a computer with only one program to function. Or as a smartphone that has a lot of apps downloaded taking up storage space and you don't use or necessarily need. However, it still uses and takes up data even if it's not a frequent app. You still run out of data. This has the same cause and effect of your subconscious versus your consciousness being aware of self-perception and reciprocal perceptions.

Conscience is consciousness of the moral right and wrong of one's own acts or motives. And conscientious is guided by one's own sense of right or wrong. You must be aware and see and believe you have ideal realistic perceptions.

You have to be clairvoyant, then you can further pursue your love path to your heart and discover your own unique desired loveprint, which is one of the main goals of this book. Also, premise.

Clairvoyant is being able to see beyond the range of ordinary perception, having the power of discerning objects not present to the senses.

Your perceptions show how your images are formed from aperture of light you cipher, transform, and translate in your language and own speed. You cannot get upset because someone cannot understand or see your perception in the same light as you. Please don't expect them to, because everyone is built different and see or interpret different. This is part of finding a connection and match with the same perceptions as you. Also the reason why people that are into the same fields and share likes, relationships last longer than from two opposite walks of life. It's not impossible if you both make it work.

Every human being is vulnerable to imperfection. Everyone is seeking truth and love but must work hard to discover it.

You can only be the best you, not the best somebody else. You can also become a great lover. You can love everything you are and have inside of you first before you can enjoy somebody else's love.

One of the hang-ups in life that we are programmed to believe is we can do anything and be the best at it. We all cannot be Lebron James and play elite basketball. However, we can be the best us and at our own skillset once we work hard daily at discovery and betterment. This is why so many people and relationships fail in life back-to-back, from us being deceived by a perceptional illusion like a desert mirage. Then some people love themselves but cannot get someone else or the world to love them back.

People make the mistake of mimicking someone else's relationship, bond, or marriage. Not out of envious motives, but from powerful perceptions of empowerment or fulfillment voids that we seek endlessly. From the ship of imagination that can take us anywhere and play on our senses, like a stimulus does. Our sights and senses can mislead us to believe from the outside looking into somebody else's posing happy ideal relationship. This is purely an envisage. We cannot see the inner depth or behind doors of their perfect public relationship. They actually can be in couples therapy or irreconcilable.

Illusion is a misleading visual image. Illusion vs. Reality. Things don't appear as they are. For example, a T.V. program is because you are being programmed. It tells you lies to tell your vision. Same with a channel that channels you and your senses and deceives you. Fiction versus Reality, which plays on your perception and takes a toll on you mentally and physically. Some people's vision is distorted, and it forces them to be antisocial and suffer from prosaic. Lacking energy because of their perception of things on the surface.

We must all understand the cause and effect of perception displays of pictures and the universal illusional fictitious web. Awareness, insight, and comprehension. Your imagery is influenced from your perception, which is linked to your sensory stimulus.

A solution how to fix your ideal perception to a loving natural one ordained by your heart is to discover your own perceptions by erasing influential imagery and reverse it, too. Be cautious and guard what you listen to, watch, and feed yourself because it sticks to your mental. Then your subconscious will play it out, feeding you perceptional cravings. You have to be inspired, focus on the details to change and cleanse your perceptional slate, your belief system, and willing to put in the hard work daily to wash your senses and give them positive energy, thoughts, and feed them. Fuel your mind with new empowerment or inspirational images, ideal designs, and love patterns to project on your subconscious, not the world's.

Remember 3 different people can watch a love story and get 3 different takes of it. One may see it different from the second one, with their own perspective. The third person may view it as their own personal love story, or ideal for true love story and continue to chase that vision. They will try to replicate and seek to implement it in every angle possible.

It's impactful in huge various areas. Some people's perception of love is simple as accepting a rose. Suspense is created by perception and can intensify situations and senses. Others see hate, fear perceptions and blinded to love. Your perception can't differentiate between sense of reality or fiction, it's up to you to be able to decipher it. Your perception is a false reality like a virtual reality gaming console.

People hold on to what they like and makes them happy. However, in discomfort zone you build and learn how and what to intake. Just like you don't stream things on your mobile device you don't like or simply not interested in because it's a waste of space and time. Your perception is the same way: you have to face it and yourself.

To face it you need to address it. Go back to your hurt, pain, and victim role you replay in your perception. Then go back to the continued dungeon you store inside and release it.

If your heart could speak, it would tell you all and reveal all. Instead, you can teach and train yourself how to feel it. Not only when you feel your heartache, pain, or distress and anxiety.

The way of thinking gives you power of wizardry. Our senses work fine for human functions but not at the speed of light. You can overcome physically, emotionally, psychologically adversity. Most people live in a box and don't go outside of the box with all this possibility of love.

You lose you when you focus on others. Not soul-searching for who you are. Finding your love essence. The easy route is a quick fix. The hard road and work is permanent and lasts. Instead of us listening to our inner heart and thoughts, however, we go to the easy, safe, mapped-out routes. We allow our mind to choose resistance and go the other way. Give yourself a challenge daily to let go of fears, etc. We all shut down and our mind tells us excuses for not working hard, progressing because it loves comfort and hates discomfort. You can win if you don't let love damage you, scar you mentally, and block your open heart. Not making the same mistake and being haunted by it and not loving or allowing life to love you back. Acceptance and validation so many lack and chase for fulfillment. Everyone doesn't see in the same language. You definitely need to find a connection and match with someone that does see in the same perceptions as you, too.

Remember, you must identify the false perceptions that you intake and shoo them away like flies, reverse it, then let it go. An artificial environment that is experienced through sensory stimuli as sights and sounds provided by an interactive T.V. program, computer program, radio/music, etc.

That certain song you hear that reminds you of someone or takes you back to a certain time and place of your life is a perceptional cue that gets triggered. The mind affects the performance. What you speak and think, you create. If you don't feel love, speak love, how can you gravitate love?

Forget negative thoughts, stop all your bad thought processes that snowball into perceptional repeat skips. If you believe your actions will produce certainty, it will. You tap into your potential and get momentum and self-fulfilling. It's having absolute certainty, focusing, and executing the action, making time to apply it. If you don't believe it works, your actions won't produce. Your action won't work unless you produce it in your head and do it as a ritual daily. You must have the intention to focus on the target areas to get the results of what you're dismissing or the relief you're seeking of love and progress.

You can't change something if you don't know it exists. Most people don't realize they have love hiccups or know how to recognize the problems and solve the troubleshoot areas. Most don't have guidance, self-discipline, or the energy. Really try to remove yourself from stressful and toxic engagement that plants bad seeds in your perception.

Perfect practice makes perfect results. However, it's progress, not perfection, that's most impactful for us breaking out of patterns and habits. You need a battle to fight in life and love. A challenge and cause to overcome. Then make it on a level of perpetual love progress all around and throughout your whole body head-to-toe. You want to have the perceptional radiant and vibrant loving glow for others to see and attract to your open, loving space and energy.

Also, it is the way you were programmed, when you say the "should" word. Like I should have trusted more, or I should have stayed with him. It's another trigger word that's a perceptional cue. You start to view that person and your mind goes back to that place and you will play on an ex and relive the hurt or the things you loved about that certain individual, which clings to your head. You need to let go of this to progress forward with so many other life choices of love, because life is full of love once you learn how to see it, feel it, and smell it. You must practice to avoid and refrain from certain words like "should" because it leaves too much open-minded space for doubt and negativity to snowball. You can't fight an opposition with an opposition. Commit and follow it.

- Chapter 3 -

"Psychology"

Now that you have identified the problem, its origin, and that it exists from your inception stages of life, then your imagery-influenced perception overall and the cause and effect with effective solutions and methodologies, next I will show you the psychology of it all together. Then you can be open to love, and later in this book I will show you, finally, how to discover your unique loveprint from the inner chambers of your thriving heart.

This chapter of psychology I will break down and show you your mental behind why you do it, how your psychology works and processes, the power of thought process, emotions manifest into feelings. Also your stained and damaged mental from imprinted perceptions and psychological effect. The frozen and stuck areas suffering from past traumas. Finally the emotional breakdown and meltdowns of our emotions with the solutions to put the emotions in check and how to reengineer your mind, perception, and subconscious to love how you are designed to.

Love isn't how you keep getting back up. Real love shouldn't fail. Love isn't an image or mission statement. Love is the strongest emotion on the planet, and it all starts inside your mental before your heart can be a receptor of love arousal.

To understand the mental you need to know what's behind your mental forces and what pushes it to work how it does.

The nucleus accumbens is the desire process in the brain. Your brain is divided into different sections with different functions. It's the cortex, frontal lobe, mid brain, cerebellum, cerebrum, and medulla oblongata. To name a few of the main brain functions, the right side of the brain controls all the left side functions and motor skills, and vice versa with the left side of the brain. From your brain stem to your front brain and cortex, it consists of brainwaves, neuros, and neurotransmitter. Your brain is basically your computer hard drive with electrocurrents.

Then you have the nervous system and the central nervous system, which is our target area where we want to tap into first and the process.

A neurotransmitter is a substance that transmits nerve impulses across a synapse. Also when you hear about a person being emotionally unstable, they refer to them as being neurotic, or a nervous breakdown being attached to the attack of the mental or emotional disorder.

It all starts in the nervous system, which is vertebrates of the brain and spinal cord, nerves, ganglia, and parts of sense organs and that receives and interprets stimuli and transmits nerve impulses.

The neurons are our cells' specialized processes, fundamental functional units of nervous tissue. Your neuros is a central unit. Axon hillock is where your brain chooses to fire or not. It's not just electric transmitters, it's also chemical.

This is why people can feel distress and emotionally off balance with traits of bipolar issues because it's a chemically infused and electric off-balance. Or you see someone have a sudden change of heart unexplainably because their mental is not aligned with the heart. The subconscious could be misleading them.

This also plays a part in the desire phase where it's intense and highly sexual in the first stage before it fades out like a falling star. It's where your dopamine attaches, which could pick up a habit or detach. Majority of us suffer from cognitive blindness. The brain doesn't stop changing; your neural data show that with your brainpower and waves.

A synapse is the point at which a nervous impulse passes from one neuron to another. All of our brain functions in response to each other, which leads to our mood and emotional response.

With post-synapse neurons and pre-synapse neurons, if it's enough charge, it may be enough to persuade the brain to do the action stimulated. It may influence the receptors to fire.

We have like 100 billion neurons in our brain, but not 100 billion neuron transmitters. The brain has different networks, and because of this physical separation, you really don't need more than a few hundred neurotransmitters.

Your axon terminal, nucleus, and neurotransmitter lie in the same mid brain area. It's several different types of neurotransmitters. The main four most of us are inflicted by are dopamine, epinephrine, serotonin, and glutemate.

Dopamine is a reward and pleasure neurotransmitter. Epinephrine is adrenaline, and the fight-or-flight response in your head. Serotonin is appetite and mood. Glutemate is the excited most in neurotransmitters.

Dopamine is a chemical receptor which tells you all your cravings and immediate satisfaction to your brain sensors. Also the dopamine receptors fall off if you're less engaged, and you will become less productive. However, if you succeed, the dopamine adds on. This is our love and like trigger cue and the spawn of addictions and habits.

Self-mastery is the key, but to be successful at that and love, you must understand your psyche mechanics first. Also you may have to apply some cognitive therapy, social support, and mindfulness meditations.

To sum it up in easier terms, how a neuro fires, pumps, and pushes. Your neurotransmitter signals a charge, lots of positive charge into the cell, letting positive ions of chemicals to axon terminal to fire the action.

Pathological is an addiction brain with an access form of dopamine. Synaptic growth, synaptic pruning, novelty, new association, increasing knowledge, consistency, efficiency, and new habits formation converts.

Addicts is really a kind of skill. The addict brain skills learn to efficiently identify and aim behavior, new skills or formation of deep habits. Also our primitive egotistic inner trouble desires of sexual or anything taboo that we don't act on in reality.

Form new insights of love. Emotional appeal of a person is highlighted to the ventral striatum, ventral activation. Falling in love cue triggers dopamine to process info and rehearsing pattern. In the striatum, falling in love causes addiction, too. Some people may be addicted to the sex or simply the pleasurable endorphins released in the brain from a physical connection versus emotional and spiritual, which people often mistake for love.

Behavioral addiction changes the ways of the brain. It's also gray matter density abnormalities. Why is it so hard to stop? Psychotherapy helps with the brain. Strong attraction, repetition, deep learning is not a set path. Getting trapped, ego depletion can't control it.

The cue trigger phase is perception, imagining, sent to your mid-brain and striatum creates craving. The prefrontal cortex starts planning and strategizing. Then relate to your motor cortex and plan of action. Then when it's over, it's often loss, shame, depression, and anxiety, which makes you want more. You get relief, learning, then loss. So you build it up for months, weeks, or years, time after time, and that developing emotion habit, a learned habit.

That's synaptic pruning. Dopamine focuses on the craving, the delay discounting which equals the now appeal. The perceived value is dopamine, and is seeking immediately award, which immediate goal outweighs the rewards of future goals.

Cues are everywhere. It's hard to suppress and control cognitive control of the brain. It doesn't work to just say no, avoid it instantly. It's better to rethink and rephrase to reevaluate. Gets determined to stop.

The PFC–Judgement, Striatum–Attraction, and Mid-Brain–Dopamine. Now appeal, this addiction and this type of love in this process in addiction is harmful. Where your attached and loving for you projections and immediate rewards of self-satisfaction versus pure wholeheartedly. It's more like a mental impulse you suffer from indirectly, not being conscious of it.

Where people think they have a disease and can't help it. If people look at it as they have an illness or a disease to justify their problems with these addiction treatment centers based solely on disease model as intervention 12-step methods. Saying you are powerless and give it over to God, addiction is chronic, and do what they tell you.

Which it fails addicts and causes people to be medical treatments as primary intervention, rendering you powerless and your belief models, which is considered highly problematic.

Neurological disease where one gene out of whack inside of you, which creates behavior disorders. Love evolutions vs. nature. The amygdala is fear and anger in the brain's neurosystem. Sometimes stuff that goes on in your body will go on in your head, too. And vice versa. The 2 influence each other's psychology and physiology. The biology of human social behavior.

Everybody has categories, boundaries inside their head, like running miles under 4 minutes and comparing measurement to rules. It's memory we take the categories and break it down easier in mental. Taking continua and breaking it into pieces is easier to handle and remember that. Thinking in categories makes it easier for us. However, when we set up boundaries or the mental walls in our head, we can't see the differences from sounds and the things we need to, creating self-sabotage blockage indirectly. When you pay too much into category thinking, you don't see the big picture.

Remember, your subconscious mind works in pictures. Your dreams work in pictures. You must reprogram if your subconscious is pulling you backwards or in a neutral position and not projecting you in a forward progress.

Neuropharmacology manipulates neurotransmitters, find out function or for disease. Increase or decrease the syntax neurons. Strength syntax response, force neurotransmitter to linger in receptor or reuptake. It's proteins to repack or reform in vessels. Neurotransmitters, they can be degraded after they're used up like dopamine receptors.

How to predict neuropathology? It's hard. You can't see people's neurowaves inside their brain. Dopamine may increase or decrease in motor skills or other areas. You could see adverse side effects.

Convince, captivate, create, correct, and collect. Reverse engineering is a method used to disassemble or analyze in details in order to discover concepts involved in manufacturing. We cannot be enervated, weak in mind or body if you're seeking to change and break your bad habits so you can obtain love and lasting relationships. Your willpower needs to be tested around designed circumstance and cause for greatness and self-betterment.

Habits are compound interest of choices we make. Habits that are immediate outcomes are favorable vs. long-term immediate gratification. Each time you embody writing, you establish yourself as a writer. Each behavior casts enough votes to the person you want to become. Habits desire the dream person you become.

Reading is a metahabit. If you find a great book, read it twice. Reading is therapeutic and helps your brain learn anything possible. If you don't rise to the levels of your goals, you will fall in love with your new system.

How long it takes to build a new habit? Some say 66 days. It will become automatic in time. However, you need to put in your reps/practice and brain will automate with your subconscious. You must be conscious with awareness.

Love is what's fused into the world and helps it go around. Everyone is entitled to it. Humans have a desire to connect and demand love—instantaneously. It's going to be more critics in your love story, and want to turn it into a psychodrama. You must invert yourself.

Most of us, we are lonely, suffer from boredom, and crave connections and social status. Learn to understand psychology first. Not desired effect that we don't need. Our minds are sick from all the bad habits and influential social norms we pick up. So we continue to hurt each other and being selfish.

People treat love like money: they're lousy with it, inconsiderate, no regards. The love of money is not a fashion; it's real and unguarded treated any way because it comes and goes. Spin it and on to the next. Some may even feel mentally broken, and emotionally broken with spirit and nature.

Controlling emotional impulse intensification process. Confused, distressed, anxious, nervous, excited are all emotions inside that may be blocks or intrigue or motivate you.

Love is also an emotion and you need to be emotionally stable in the falling in love phase. Else it alters the psychological effect and could have a negative toll on your relationship, ending in short-term irreconcilable differences.

Your thoughts manifest into feelings, and your emotions also manifest into feelings. Your feelings manifest into your nervous system. This is why you're feeling depressed or emotionally sick. It shows through your face and body language. If you believe you're sick, you really convince yourself and body to become sick.

If you choose to be positive, people will see you as positive and you will feel it, too. You will feel an aura with your crown chakra and your heart chakra will both be radiant with love and a bright color glow. Create a structure and process of positive thoughts. Little tweaks and adjustments go a long way. You have to passionately seek it like love.

Stop dead in your negative thoughts, emotions, feelings, and alter your mood. Tell yourself the opposite with good positive empowering thoughts. Keep cramming that into your head like a song until it sticks, and stimulate your brain to stabilize your new mood. Your brain will catch it sooner or later and start to believe, then manifest it into reality. It's the same way with any hurtful situation or financial. If you tell yourself, "It's okay, I'm okay...my heart's still beating and I'm still breathing," then take 3 deep breaths to let go and exhale all the hurt and emotional distress in your body and head. It's a reset process that enables a method for a fresh start.

Vulnerability hurts us and leaves us open to be hurt and preyed on. To become tough, we have to let go of the weak links in you. Find the bad connections, release it, and make good connections. Healthier choices, and conscious choices, lead to healthier love and relationships.

There is no drug to help you get over love. Maybe the love loss you suffered from was not your real matching loving components from your design loveprint? Maybe that relationship was meant to show you that you still have to find and align yourself with a mental and emotional tune-up to get your biorhythm in sync with heart rate.

See, a lot of us are so lost within the wave of the world that we forget from our natural powers and tools we possess as babies. Not only in the first 5 years do we learn how to walk, talk, run, and laugh. We have a tremendous sense of touch, taste, and feel. It was part of our inceptional developmental stages for primal survival traits.

When a baby is born, it cries until it is cradled into the mother's chest. This is because the baby could feel the mother's heartbeat and know her biorhythm from the womb with sense of sound. It is proven scientific fact that babies can hear inside the mother's stomach. Some mothers read to their babies, play music, and fathers even lie on her stomach and talk to it, too.

This is the same way how it works and sensational effect once you find someone else's biorhythm and beats in sync with same heart tune as yours does! That's where the matchmates of magical love ferments. I will further elaborate later on in this book how to discover that, too.

Which is an important antidote for ego fatigue? They have to own other goals only you make, not people hand to you. Help them envision a future and get out eternal present tense. See life as a narrative—past, present, and future. Where you come from and going.

Remember the power of mantras' positive effect to your psychology. Telling yourself positive things like "You can, you can" and "Just do it" repeatedly helps you deal with your emotions, feelings, and alter your brain to change to a more positive mood.

Most relationships are starters and don't kill us. The mind doesn't know false sense of reality. It projects you to survive. If you get a bad seafood experience sick, the body won't let you eat it again and scare you.

It's different avenues to people's hearts. Hears to different people's ears and used different words for people to process. Love isn't impossible for people with different languages. It's us that creates language barriers with our partners. Where one person becomes mute to the other, then relationship falls like the weather. If your vibrations are clear and entuned, then it doesn't matter what foreign language they speak. Jesus used parables to connect and communicate with different people directly to their hearts.

Our individual capacities being empathetic understanding human nature, superior and social sense. Look for patterns through people's nature. It's how to recognize toxic people before you attach to them by the hip and heart. People should be helpmates, not hurtmates. Similar in terms but different in outlooks. Our shared values and alignment.

Love is vital and value one's self-knowledge. Know thyself, love yourself, learn thyself. Even the jealous, envy, and emotional patterns you plant in your head to evolve. All falls inside the realm of mental health. Cognitive skills and self-awareness are a key element. Conflict and grief stem from inaccurate communication in partners and what they really feel. We don't know how to relay and deliver the same context that's in our heads effectively to our partner. Miscommunications can be avoided if you learn to stop and listen, intake, and be patient.

The feelings of emotions can also make you resourceful and fueled with passion. However, if you let go of the emotion attached, the addiction is gone. Social media is changing our persona and shrinking our world around us. Social now is characterized by friends and friendship status. You need to be who you are called to be, not how society calls you to be or program to love with a social prototype loveprint. Suitability and satisfaction are the biggest sources of discernment.

People don't learn to communicate or use their communication channel to the right frequency where people can reciprocate and grasp without discrepancy. They don't develop it clearly. We live in a life in the opinion of others. Regret is living with judgement. When you deny love and don't receive other people's love. The grandness of endless/unlimited love. Stand in front of the mirror and give yourself love, admire your inner heart, not just your outer physical appearance. Speak loving things and watch your heart and smile crack open.

You get bored of being the victim, depression, and anxiety, then you heal and get over it. You get tired, wipe your eyes, exhale, and you want to love and find love. You won't have an overnight success on love, but a strong practice loving routine daily.

Everyone needs to allow themselves space and stillness, the answer of love. Within creating time out and space, we have healing and joy, not an agenda. We have to give up all our resistance and fear to love, change, and let go to be amazing and break through. It takes a lot of courage to let it through. We are on limited time. Don't live life and die heartbroken with regrets.

Sometimes you have to surrender and trust. Nature shows you what you want, wants you, too, if you don't get in the way of it and stop it with blockage from your mental. Courage is always rewarded, but it has to start with an effective initiative. You bring so much heart to your life, work, and others. Running your memory and access your memory with growth and positive energy flow to happiness and places using your cognitive awareness principles. Then apply healing nutrition love.

If you don't acknowledge your emotions and feelings, you are not aware of it, you cannot have feelings and problems stemming from them. You need to express yourself and talk them out. It's very therapeutic.

When you keep stuff in, it causes you pain and snowballs, doing so much damage. Express your emotional hurt as closely as possible. You can't get no resolution after all these years and past relationships all bottled in. Even if it's just saying it out loud or to yourself in the mirror, you don't have to have someone to confide in to clear out your emotional distress, hangups, and hurts.

You have to understand the psychology. We like familiar and usually people resist what's unfamiliar. Most find guys like their dad or first boyfriend because he was a good dad, or abusive, or an alcoholic. It's, again, your first programmed system of love perceptions. Your mind doesn't care if it's good or bad, wrong or right. Your mind is like a sponge and will let it in. Especially your subconscious.

If you say to yourself good things, your mind believes it and takes it in. Praise yourself. If you do it to someone else, it can be a form of manipulation. Eventually it becomes familiar because you get used to it. You can make anything familiar with self-praise. No self-doubt!

With rejection, it won't kill you, but you may think it would. Feeling inferior of bullying people trying to hurt your feelings, play on your emotional fears, pride, or vibrant energy to diminish you.

Don't let it in, and it will not work. People who are so critical always have criticism with themselves. You don't have to be around it or accept like a gift. So don't let it in, and it cannot hurt you. Keep rejecting it. Illness just isn't caused by disease, it's the feelings that can't find their expression, and tears will eventually cause your organs to weep.

Every word you say is a blueprint that your mind is trying to put in perspective and process it into a reality. Stop saying you can't find love or you gave up on love! Love is life and all around us. Love is electric and vibrant. We all have a natural love sphere around us like pheromones.

The problem is we disconnect our own love plug from the server. So others cannot truly see your love sign fueled by electricity shining bright. Your love light shines bright and will attract certain people, maybe even your matchmate. Just like insects attracted to light in the pitch dark. It's the law of love and attraction. It's inevitable.

How do you cut your switch back on? How do you keep your switch on? How do you even find your love switch? It's all within your mental. What you do, who you are, and what you say. First, start by clearing the clutter out internally. All negative thinking, worrying, others' negative energy, or criticism, self-doubts, and acceptance/rejection. Don't move the furniture around trying to hold onto it up there. You must throw it out to clear and free yourself and past pain and hurts of emotions and bad habit choices.

Self-health, self-healing, appreciation, and gratitude. Only you can fix and work on you with effort, awareness, and acknowledgement. Growth and betterment will catch on and your subconscious will steer the wheel. Then will give and feed your brain power with more healthy cognitive dopamine of great loving things to enjoy and forecast. It's your belief system. One day and step at a time. Life comes at you, all you can do is love in the present moment, not dwelling on the future, stuck in the past, and worrying about your biological clock. Especially for if you are more of an introvert person.

It's important to remember thoughts create reality and tools in creating process. The old you is comfortable because you built in status quos. You can get high motivation and positive energy dealing with the conscious, but only subconsciously control your daily habits. What we believe determines what we convince ourselves on a subconscious level become your reality. What we look for is what we find. What we believe is determined what becomes true. Our light is what we make from. Break through encrusted mind script that takes years to build. You must rescript the core beliefs of what your perceptional modified by your brain to be true. Your subconscious is welded with your programs of future.

An effective solution and tool to program your conscience to bring and form the visionary session. Take an exclusive 5 minutes time out to rest and relax. Listen to yourself breathe, focus on your breath, and further relax. Inhale and exhale 5x. This is a relax exercise that puts your body in an alpha state. Induce an alpha brain wave state in 45 seconds.

Next, place an image and a feeling, or a very specific event to help you. Or a positive image from the past and bring in your conscious a goal that becomes energized and into your subconscious to alter your reality. A sensory image, pics or words, or a feelings, a taste sense.

Open your eyes and tell yourself that I now know how to love, and now I can receive love, too! Once you tell yourself that, it affirms it, and subconscious plays on it to make it into a reality. Believe you deserve it, and not guilty about it. Remove from subconsciousness all the automated programs our parents, peers, and society planted in your psychology.

By thinking love, seeing love, believing love, you will feel love, and eventually fall in love. You literally have psychological love cues and receptors. Chemicals and chemistry with your biology. Like lovemaking, its intense focus, mind, body, heart stimulate simultaneously.

- Chapter 4 -

"Attraction"

What do you attract? Who do you attract? Is it traits, your patterns, or preference? What energy you put out is what energy you attract and pull inwards, from negative vibes to positive, radiant, glowing aura vibes aligned with your chakras.

Everything that looks good to you isn't always good for you. A lot is about right choices versus life choices. This chapter of attraction is a focal point of your troubleshoot areas. Effective choices and hurt/pain self-inflicted decision patterns of attractions.

Love is blind, but it is a certain algorithm and vibrant attraction to it also. It's a main element to be induced to produce the right matchmate you're attracting and the one you were meant and born to attract with the universe.

We all fight and struggle, since birth, Earth's gravitational pull and pulls of life itself. Must detoxic and clean slate free and give the universal law of attraction a makeover. Then you can have the love of attraction.

Love is law, too. Your choices of partners should be options. Don't mistake choice for connection. Just because you choose a partner does not mean it's a chosen connection there, too. You could be attracting the wrong things and people with huge warning signs that you choose to ignore and further explore. Blinded by the shiny infatuation instead of chemistry impulse of your inner loveprint.

Some attraction is misled for simply admiration. Or you can be attracted to what the world is doing or following that's a hot topic and be whirlpooled directly into it.

Connection vs. chemistry. Anyone can create a work team, soccer team, or whatever cause and have instant chemistry flowing from all angles. Entuned with the mission, goals, and task. It's either right chemistry or wrong chemistry, and then someone that's holding back with wrong chemistry is kicked out of the group or fired from the team. Chemistry can confuse you and be mistaken or tricky even for connection. It's not connection.

You can be vibing with a new person and high energy flowing in a positive manner and even have same interests, but that's just a good environment, not a solid connection. You can create chemistry with people naturally. It's one of our social nature habits we form and a survival mechanism.

Now a true connection is internal. Something you feel from the inside out, not the outside in because of looks. It's deeper than the surface. A connection is not a hook-up or something that you both have in common. It's just like the interpretation of peace. Some people say they need peace and quiet. Peace isn't no place or environment. Real peace is your state of mind, and you having peace in your head regardless of your environment or conditions.

To make a true connection, you must be open to what you attract. If you're emotionally unstable, you may attract that or the opposite. Once you attract the opposite and they notice your emotional distress is problematic, they flee and you can miss or block your blessings. We were built for love and to love others and the world around us, too. You don't want to miss out on a better relationship and lover.

A lot of people's problems in this troubleshoot area are they shoo people away like flies because of their past relationship, emotional distress, and hang-ups post-breakup. It's an attraction stage where you may not be looking for love or a mate, but you still let off pheromones and attracting people. Especially with men because guys love a challenge and to compete. Don't nobody want an easy catch for a lifetime mate. You can have a face of apathy, expressionless, and that freak-off look, with arms folded expressing negative body language and vibes. Someone still tries to make you smile and attempt to sweep you off your feet, if not simply move you off your square. Love is always in your atmosphere.

Once someone attempts to break through your walls and breach your barriers all around you, and you deny them, later when you go home and wind down, you begin to think back and start getting emotional from your self-sabotage attraction flaws and begin to cry yourself asleep again. Weep!

It's not too bad because when you cry, you also release emotional distress hormones. You can flush it all out, then get your emotions in check and out of that slump stage.

Remember, with break-ups, past traumas, and bad habits, you need time to release and let go, then the healing process. Holding it in will end up with you suffering emotionally and can possibly affect physical health, too.

You can be emotionally incarcerated. It's some people emotionally free that's actually incarcerated, versus people free but emotionally incarcerated inside. You must learn how to process your emotions and to deal with them. Master your emotions by daily steps I showed you in previous chapters.

However, there is also a recent popular tapping method used to redirect and stop your emotions, anxiety, and feelings by stimulating the acupuncture points like the Chinese design with the needles for pain and disease, except this is simply tapping quick solutions by hand. No needles involved. The science behind tapping is to manifest speaking and auto mechanics in the brain, sending an electrical signal through the body to the brain to change your thought process of emotional distress and anxiety. At work, in relationships, or wherever, you can use this method as a quick hack to put your emotions back into check.

How do you apply it effectively? First, you tap with your hands on the acupuncture points. Like the karate chop part of your hand. The orbit points around your eye, the tip of eyebrow, side of eye, and under the eye. The top of your crown on your head. The collarbone one inch under, and the side of armpit by the rib.

Do a set-up statement for tapping process. Bring up all emotions you want to clear or may be experiencing at the moment. Start tapping and say, "You're going through a situation temporarily, and you love and accept yourself!" You can say and address whatever you like. Just make sure it's followed by greatness and loving statements. You need to bring up your emotions, enable to clear it and all the anxiety, too. Give a voice to the problem. This will trigger your brain to ignite and switch your emotional distress and problems very quickly, giving a solution for relief.

Everyone has a go-to and how they deal with stress and emotions directly or indirectly. Mainly indirectly. May include porn, sex, binge eating/drinking, and abusiveness. Or excessive chain-smoking heavy.

Don't burn out chasing things and the wind with false attractions. Life is too short to not have or find true love. Live from your heart, love and watch how free you become and wholehearted.

It's the right balance, complement each other without conflict. With a real connection, we embrace our weakness and don't exploit each other playing on it like a thumbscrew.

Everyone latches on to the person they think is too good to be true. You act on a way to fuel someone's fears. We're not entuned to what we are doing wrong, stuck in the wave of the world and competitive workplace, that we ignore or neglect to create time and space for our partners. It's no depth anymore and becomes remote and automated.

People argue about spouses or mates not appreciating them or being priority. We contribute to make it more problematic and being effortless. Also, when we see sex on the brain, we don't process right and refocus, evaluate, and understand. We need to express it and articulate it. Fine-tune how you express things and learn a way to say things people can grasp and interpret. Hear people and don't be so quick to react. Listen, process, then speak. Not emotional responses.

Connection is key and deeper than initial shock attraction that you like or love about them. If you are in a very emotional healthy place and space, you will attract that for someone to connect and possibly match.

Opposites do attract and it exists if two people click and feel intense feelings right away. You could've missed a beat and blinded to your love cue that wasn't in sync. You know if it's real potential or rationalize. Now you get stuck and try to make it work, when you knew it wasn't a true connection from the beginning of the relationship. With tons of regret and wasted time and potential, which the cause of this further alienates yourself and lapses your emotions into a perpetual cycle state. You must conquer your emotions first before you can achieve self-mastery successfully. However, you must know thyself and learn thyself before you can find yourself.

The exercise of the inner sight through the third eye is a process of attraction, too. You have an inner superpower to align and stimulate your super chakras aura and atoms. Everything in the universe is a source of atoms and molecules. Just like an atomic bomb utilizing the energy released by splitting the atom, the energy of attraction is vibrant and all over. It's a natural vibration of atoms or molecules and the very source of all our beings. Even the energy vibration of the world is at its highest in the past 10 years. It feels like magic and your attraction is absolutely your inner connection.

Protons in the nucleus of an element is not a set number, but it is universal source, too, all around us. Protons are an energy force radiant or nuclear-like attraction. Protons can force together and lose a lot of energy versus protons that distant stay strong force and energy. It's the work needed to be done to make the force, meaning like the universal scientific law on protons, some people's attraction can force you to lose energy and your natural vibration. That's what you must catch and distinguish in your paradigm.

Also your inception and perceptional attraction may be deluded, wrong for you, or not in your decree. You must absorb something else or continue to be confused. Just like being typecast in

Hollywood, you can be typecast in your attraction for one single role and image. Colorism, you can be color-blind and only attract in black and white. This is a contrast you must be aware of, break and see through prisms. You can't have a limited cultivation of perception attraction. Wasted energy can be used for creativity.

Do not be reclusive or resistant to universal attraction of love. Never let someone else narrate your attraction of love and life. Do not stunt your own growth, you can't have a limited perception. Don't let people's attractions convert you and yours. Delivery is key. Don't hold on to images you were attracted to keeping relationships going because of family's sake and others. Please, don't dim your light and vibration for them versus what your spirit wants to be.

When people come together, it is to grow and love to the best ability. Most of all for betterment. That's the ideal of what you are aiming to attract to make a positive connection for a lifetime loving mate. If growth stopped and people's paths diverted without no renewal, you learn to separate or move on. Worrying is a mental repeat fear of what's to happen. This all can be avoided from the very start if your attraction is aligned and the right vibration stemming from your own loveprint. You must shift and grow in your relationships, always forward progress and attractions. Mediocrity always attacks excellence. People afraid to be ridiculed or afraid to fail, then still crave acceptance and validation of others.

The ego don't know we block out all the love abundance of the world and our attraction out of fear and uncertainty. We only live a fraction of our life in a sure reality because of our belief system and automated repeated programs planted on our subconsciousness passed-down norms from our parents, and it's learned, too, from society.

Attraction, you can left-swipe it out of your head or counter it. How you're becoming in this new goal, you become vibrant and people feel the wave of your vibration and magnetize attract to it. You must not let negative attraction stick to you, with you, or in you because it will consume your life aura. They can send toxic energy through our body temples. You can't be territorial, else your attraction will be scripted and limited.

Ego is what protects you during evolvement. Its first job is to protect, but we have to transcend the ego for it not to become crazy. People grow from two ways: crisis or insight. Your pain pushes you until you are pulled by a vision. Once you get your structure down, stabilize it. Shapeshift, take energy from that, and connect a feeling, vision, and description of it. Once again it will become an attraction manifesto. Don't procrastinate.

The ability to attract the image of the perfect pattern to be precipitated, to see the vision of a project complete, to draw a mental picture, to retain it and fill it in with light, spiritual aura, love, and joy are keys to the science of attraction. Based on visualization of a perfect idea which then becomes a magnet that attracts the creative energies of your loving spirit to your being to fulfill the love pattern held in mind.

Do not mistake affection for attraction. If you're seeking affection, you may get sexual attraction, which always ends up in messy turmoil situations and plays a major factor in troubleshoot area spaces. Sexual attractions are distractions from real love with heart and mind versus the lusting of the unchaste body. They are polluting the attraction of their own world, as well as the attraction of the Earth. This is where the pollution starts in your head and offsets your heart's biorhythm, from confusing sex for love. A cold case of lust of love. It's just like the lone wolf disguised in sheep's clothing scenario. It needs to be repudiated inside.

Break your attraction habits and practice of scarcity, fear, and protectiveness. You cannot continue to be in the reptilian brain and really think that's enough. You need to be vibrational worth and vibrational alignment to how it works. The universe will bring more love, joy, happiness, and vibrational opportunity to express more to you. Or else you can have a physical restraint manifest.

Finally there is also such a thing as a spiritual attraction, and a spiritual connection, too. Not in religiously, but in awareness, consciousness, and your inward being. A real spiritual love connection and attraction is vibrant and love felt in every cell and molecule in your body. It's a radiant spiritual aura that will have all 7 chakras in harmony inside to where people will see you from the outside glowing. It's contagious how the spiritual love is so divine through you and the universe once you find that connection, especially with a matchmate and potential spouse. It's very evident.

You also can attract friends that's strictly platonic love without sexual desires. Divine friendships are priceless, if you can be with others without gossiping, or tearing people down, etc., and have stabilized foundation. Attraction is mental energy that projects speech, perceptions, and actions. It's law.

- Chapter 5 -

"Loveprint"

Loveprint is your DNA blueprint of love. What's built and encrypted in the chambers of your heart. What sparks your heart to electrify that burning desire of love and that pumping thud of rhythmic entuned love. Your heart doesn't just pump adrenaline to your head, it also pumps and fires up love throughout your whole body head-to-toe, and endorphins in your head and libido system.

I believe everyone has their own unique loveprint, just like everyone has their own individual thumbprint. You must learn, discover, and access yours, too, and its own unique design. The biorhythm of it, and what keys to your heart you're missing for someone or possible matchmate to open a hidden chamber of your ultimate and infinite love secret source that lies at the heart dormant, which need to be active and open to pump love endlessly and euphoric. Start a path to your divine love design.

How do you access and cultivate it? How do you break up the blockage layer of your heart so love can flow from your crown chakra to your heart chakra with energy vibration to your cosmic awareness?

Being committed to your loveprint wholeheartedly, not self-sabotage or derailed because you go back to what you know and comfort zone. Most people are scared of love, and what it does to them or did to them in the past. They can't control their emotions and hate it, or afraid to find love because of their careers and life path goals.

The solution is discovery, ignite, imply, then redirect your loveprint. Must be able to recognize if you're walking in someone else's love boots or your own. Watching someone else's love story play or starring in your own epic love story is your focal point. It's not only a cognitive shift, it's shaping the heart and making it connect back to your senses and sensitivity of love.

Your head is disconnected from your heart, hindering you from your designed loveprint. Once you are aware and recognize the disconnect, you can begin to fix and redirect it. Most people already feel it in their heart that things aren't right and there is an obvious void that something is missing deep in your heart and relationship. Its thirst drives you to crave fulfillment.

You can train yourself how to listen to your heart versus your head. When you follow your heart, it will feel it and righteous versus you having a gut feeling. A gut feeling is an instinct, not an impulse. However, your head is wired to feed your gut and fuel all cravings. Your loveprint is the craving of your true heart design and identity.

Most people's heads don't agree with their hearts and so out of touch that they believe their heads and not their hearts. The head barricades the heart and gives you self-doubt and pushes your mind on fantasy mode of someone else's love story and loveprint. Its ideal is to further distance the heart from head because it's afraid the heart's clear conscience and being the seat of your soul will do the more righteous and natural things.

What's good for your head is not always good for your heart. Your head will crave for junk food, fast food, but it's not good for your heart and health. It will tell you not to exercise or work out regularly because of the laziness in the mental procrastination process of our minds. The human mind is thousands of years old and is our primal surviving mechanism that's used to living in fear and playing it safe. However, we have evolved as primates on this Earth, so we must learn not to let our head drown out our heart's desires and cravings.

We all know our heart's intuition naturally. The brain signals doubt or fear to ignore it. Or it simply sends a perceptional imagery of someone else's loveprint to deceive you to further trick your heart. You must see the patterns because they're all right there in front of you. Every person has behavior patterns and traits they do daily like a ritual.

Meditating and listening to your breathing to relax, then focusing on your heartbeat and rhythm after clearing out your head and thoughts, will help you align better with your loveprint to find where that wire is disconnected at from your heart to your head. Your head doesn't override your heart, but the subconscious lets it every time and further project for you to disconnect. It will even make you think you would be better alone and without love of this world. Your head will overanalyze, but you need to learn to let your heart start to analyze. You cannot program your heart like the mind. Your true heart will never deceive or mislead you. It's your heart of hearts.

This is why you hear someone entuned versus impulsive say, "Let me sleep on it!" because when they sleep on something, they clear their heads to be on a conscious level to tell their minds to shut off and up while they tune in to listen to their heart's decree. Once you sleep and become into that alpha state mind zone and that deep level of sleep consumes you, your biorhythm is at its peak. Your heart is singing, drumming, or crying if you can practice to learn how to relax, cut off your mind meditation until you feel the pull of your heart and gravitation of love vibrations through you. That special feeling and aura over your sphere of love is truly spiritual and you'll feel your aligned chakras glowing.

I asked a girl in high school what is her definition of love just out of mere curiosity...she said the movie *The Notebook* and the movie *A Bronx Tale*. I scratched my head, lost and confused. However, I did see she did have an influence of a movie's love story that she projected to decree as hers, too.

The next year when I moved out of town, I asked an older girl that was out of high school and worked as a supervisor at a telemarketing company, What is her definition of true love? She said...someone that loves her, takes care of his family, and a hard worker. I frowned. Not in a stink face, but more like I had a bad taste in my mouth because what she had described was basically her dad. I knew her father personally, too.

Of course, both girls' answers weren't from their hearts or their own loveprints. Their answers were from their mental inceptions and perceptions, which clearly were projected in them visually and audibly.

If your true loveprint is not there, it will lead to the inevitable break-up, love loss, or infidelity, and an illusion of love. If you've ever seen someone crushed after a devastating divorce or break-up after a long time, once they found out they were living a lie and it was false love, and not their own actual loveprint they were living, that it was actually their mom's, partner's, or society's love story. They planted with a false sense of heartshock. Really, your heart is relieved and your head is more emotional because it was your subconscious loveprint that was programmed and not your heart's. It is bad and something you don't want to experience or see your loved ones or kids go through. Even though so many of us suffer from it.

Do not let your mind be the paradox of your loveprint. Allow your heart to be your trusted advisor. Remember, you must learn how, know how, and understand how to love yourself before the world or someone else knows the value of your heart. Don't let the digital era of the world digitalize your heart and the definition of your heart, which it already does to the world's mind of people that are disconnected and glued to the screens of their smartphones. You must develop a smart heart and take daily steps and time out each day to work on hearing your heart, meditation, and clearing the clutter and noise out of your head. You can become a master at meditation and tuning into your heart's loveprint with practice and dedication. To know thyself, you must know thy heart.

People can use sex in the power of persuasion to further delude your heart's desire from brain dopamine, to control people's mind and actions. However, this is manipulation and not real love. These are the toxic people in relationships you need to disconnect and steer clear from. The only thing you can control is your thoughts and actions. Do not let someone trigger your emotions to connect your passion with feelings to your authentic loveprint. Once you see people's patterns and know their habits, you can know how to detect, avoid, and block. It's a private independent process that you cannot let your passion triggers or trust patterns of your set routines manifest in your head for sustainability or a foundation. Or look at it as tangible love goals and look to earn partner respect. You must alienate people that further you to disconnect from your loveprint. Your alarm trigger needs to kick in. Certain actions need to be able to take place to keep things intact on your loveprint. To maintain the reality of your loveprint and bioengineer of it. Versus your mind's false sense of reality of your ideal loveprint. That's a combination of a dominant influence of others and imagery. Isolate to reverse primary to secondary flip of your mind's loveprint. Your heart's loveprint needs to be primary, not secondary.

Love hacks and quick fixes are only temporary short-term fixes, breaking long-term further damaging something else. They tap into emotional connections to mislead you to keep using their services and apps. You want to avoid all these quick-skip solutions because anything in life and love takes time to develop.

Also, the mind can trick your emotions to trigger your feelings with a false sense of reality of a perceptional heartbreak. When your heart flutters, skips a beat, sinks, speed-races, or butterflies in your tummy is because you're falling into a perceptional pitch of love from someone else's love narrative. However, again, you must remember your heart and true loveprint is a match and would not ever deceive or mislead you, long as you're omniscient having infinite awareness, understanding, and insight. You must distinguish heart waves from brainwaves. Rewire the heart like a triple bypass and connect.

You cannot find true love without trust or trusting yourself. It's image and it's truth. You see the imagery in the mirror, but under that image is the truth and true you. You need to drop and forget about your persona and that mirror image. You need to personify and your truth reflect your true loveprint. Your authentic organic self.

It is not just the surface, it is more layers deeper in you. Most people don't know their potential and loveprint exist because they have emerged and adopted someone else's.

Once you're conscious of your loveprint, you will start to see it, breathe it, achieve it, and believe it. It will manifest in your heart in a vibrant victorious triumphant thud of a beat. The overwhelming feeling you will have once you learn how to listen to your heart and discover your true loveprint in the essence of the chambers of your heart, how it beats, what it beats for, and how to nurture it and reflect the love inside it outwards to be reciprocated, it will spark and electrify throughout the whole body, stimulating all your senses better than coffee or a drug.

- Chapter 6 -

"Levels of Love"

It is levels to love. It's elements and principles of love, too, that you must be aware of. It's various types of love and the parts they play—good, bad, manipulative, controlling, for granted, abuse, power, etc. Levels to spot, recognize, drop, and defend yourself and heart. However, treachery is always vicious and gut-wrenching, so you shouldn't be misled or deceived by it. Love shouldn't be on high demand, it should be natural. I will show you the different types of love on each of their levels. You may have these problems or suffer from them. Or simply can be aware to know the difference once they present at your front door or pop up trouble in your relationship.

Most people sought out to find and conquer love like the 7 seas. Remember, you must first know and understand love emotional elements and love triggers/cues and love principles. Then how to love someone else precipitated, pure and sincere wholeheartedly.

Love is built on integrity and values, respecting someone else's space, a strong, loving connection that vibration is ongoing. Not manipulation, greed or taking advantage of someone else's values. Most people content on love is illogical. Not all love is amicable, meaning peaceful/friendly.

It's love contingencies that require multiple elements of love. Some people are puppet master of the contingency of love. Some people look at the world through rose-colored lenses. A sexual love diversion could turn emotional quickly into a train wreck. From casual sexual diversion to dreams of a certain future to love.

Neither one of the couples understand the gravity of love or their chemical off-balance. Entwined and entangled in love. Intense lust that rocks and vibrates your limbic system. Passionate sex in earlier years of relationships filled with deep, passionate lovemaking fade and magic wears off and out. Then it feels like your love burns out and your connection, too.

Intuitive is great in love, but competition is not necessary and could actually damage love, making your partner feel timid or insecure. You can love everything about someone, but have bad chemistry, too, without no growth or the paradox of finding that balance.

A cocktail of lust, passionate lovemaking, intense dark passion, and every single thing in between. Most couples settled into sex or lovemaking as a routine without innovation. Some like the black magic love, they love the actual dark nature, not evil dark, but the deeply intense, thriving love.

Most people don't see their mortality and lack of freedom, they see unlimited sky and unlimited future. You cannot trust but be in love and have an emotional connection from the very first time they saw partners. Time passing could change them both. Some don't diminish their love, but diminish their fidelity. Some don't have no tangible explanation other than passage of time, basic needs not met in a long-term relationship, or normal human consumption. Long-term love and monogamy slip over time. Nowadays the average person in this tech fast-paced world doesn't like waiting more than 16 seconds for a website to load, to wait on hold with customer service, or to wait in traffic besides at a traffic light. So just imagine most recent relationships' time lapse. You must be careful of who you're loving and what building blocks foundation of love structural format organize in your timeline sequence. Time is definitely of your value.

It's why some long love affairs fade eventually like stars is because it was not set up and aligned with their loveprint from initial inception periodic table.

If you're telling people you want to be their friend forever disengaged, if you do not like people around you, and be unhappy, toxic, it will have an effect at home life. Less engaged. People work a third of their lives and still don't know a third of their heart or partner's love decree.

One face-to-face conversation is better than an email or text because people may read it or take it wrong. Especially if you're an introvert, which break-ups and miscommunication over text messages is very harmful and heartfelt to people. It's a devastating effect on people at an alarming rate. It's unhealthy, and digital dementia plays a huge factor. The burnout culture.

Focus on own fulfillments first. Figure out where your strength and passion lies and act on it. Share ideas, passion, and take risks on something new to apply. Life challenges and love goals. A third of America suffers from anxiety or depression. External circumstances we cannot control, we need to move on if things are not working.

People think sex would cure love blues, love, and attention to cure desired love. People want to believe a person agreed for their desire, but in their hearts it's about appeasing their partner.

If you tell a lie, you need 7 more lies to keep it covered up. Also overthinking leads to self-doubt and indecision. You need to be decisive. You must snap out of your reverie and regain control of your loveprint by turning back to the love path's design/destiny by your vibrant heart.

The irony of love. You need to ascertain what you know or do not know about love. Being brutally harsh/honest and overprotective of love. Love consequences, choices, and actions will continue to loom largely in your mind, then constrict your heart's desire love metrics because of your consciousness.

Love is not just a powerful emotion, action, and noun. It's a daily skill practice that can become naturally perfected to the recipient.

It is a huge gray area in love with the limbic system, human anatomy, and biology that's unprocessed with human psyche. Each person is unique and their own perspective, or prototype A, of what love is, or should be, and should feel like. Some ideas are unfathomable, and others put themselves in a dreamy-like state versus the real qualities of human beings make, which consist of short attention spans, boredom, curiosity, greed, envy, jealousy, hate, sexual urgency, attentiveness, attention seekers, etc. No Mr. Perfect Universe on a white, puffy cloud.

Also, the replica effect where your visual effect of X, or ideal point of choice, or prototype similarize relatable people in that specific frame and category of your ideal point of interest. You have to detect the symbols, signs, and from being stuck. Avoidance and making a change. Do not rush in or rush love, impulsive and gung-ho. Do not be a fool or fooled to rush into anything because when you rush in quick, it usually ends quick with heartache and headache. Bonds are not built overnight. It takes complacent time.

Now I will share with you other aspects, elements, and different levels of love what people experience directly or indirectly. Some people confuse for real love or simply think it's the design of their loveprint, but they're only victims that suffer from psychological and social norm perceptional delusions of love. Looking for the love in someone else before self.

If the average human gets over 50k thought processes per day, it takes 72 hours for something shocking, devastating, and problematic to get out of your head and over. A lot of people will project or point out to others what they see about themselves. Sometimes your all is not enough, sometimes it is too much. Humans always come back for love and to love.

Love's transparency, true love you can see clear through all the signs, feelings, and gratitude. Laws of attraction, what vibrations you put in is what you get out, negative or positive... birds of a feather flock together. Gravity love, the gravitational pull, attraction pulling you guys both together like the cosmos and tides the ocean created by the currents of the seas.

It is love after heartbreak, guarded, mistrust, insecurities, paranoia, and frightful. Heart-aching love, a scandal, dramatic, negative, and cheating. Dangerously in love, is limitless, love without barriers, accountability, accommodations, risky, and immoral. Emotional love is a roller coaster love, being into your feelings, and always emotionally offset. Entitlement lover feels entitled, they're obligated to be loved, loving someone less than self.

Keep in mind, the most powerful emotion ever on this Earth is love driven by passion and satisfactions. One-sided love is no reciprocation. You can actually love someone whose feelings are not mutual or accommodate yours, which beware, because most of these lovers have hidden agendas and ulterior motives, usually sexual. These are all examples and concepts of levels of love people go through or are afflicted by.

Manipulation lover is clearly taking advantage of big me, little yous, can be in many different forms and hidden agendas, masked, posers, very observant, be leery of people's intentions and motives. Eye of love is the apple of your eye, love that's only pleasing on the exterior, mere fascination versus emotional connection. Competitive lover, love is not a competition, do not exceed your love by outdoing them.

Wholehearted lover is sincere and pure with everything 110 percent of all you and vibrant energy, selfless. Love and hate is war feud once love is flipped upside down and a party is deceived or mistrust, neglect, jealousy, envy, etc., whatever triggers it. Appreciated love is having full-on appreciation and too much gratitude and attachment, which can be seen as too much emphasis and sensitive.

Attraction lover, love is blind, and true love is hard to find. This is default of a perceptional prototype that you are attracted to versus your actual loveprint. However, compatibility is key instead of people going off their ideal likes and persuasive standards, but mistake likes for love.

You have family love like from a parent, sibling, or love that you give to a child. Same as bromance category. It's a non-romantic love, more like a warm platonic love. It's simply just a beloved person. Chivalry is the love at first sight, like instantaneously, you love that person. Some people believe this is not logical and could not possibly exist, versus some who are moved by it. Impulsive love is jumping in head-first without no development stages, friendship or bond established without no Yelp reviews or evaluations. Fake love is unauthentic or fabricated love, usually with envious motives. Crazy love is indifference and contrasting flagrantly with love and nonexistent circumstances.

Then you have lovelorn, deprived of love or of a lover. Lovesick, yearning and expressing a lover's longing. Lovebirds are nesting together in the vibrant magic of electrifying brain synonymous stimulation. Lusting love, attraction based on sexual desire only. Opposites attract, biracial love becoming new norm, and race is something society puts a stipulation on and oddly taboo. However, same-sex marriages and couples are also examples of opposites attract. Absorbed love, felt like love but wore off from unrealistic. Love betrayal is cheating, infidelity, treason, or impurity of the relationship. The promiscuous lover, consisting of various sorts and partners usually to fill a void or chasing universal love. Spiteful love, to treat maliciously, annoy, offend with ill will, or a wish to anger or frustrate. A love loss is something flagrant and unforgivable. Baby love is in love with the kids after birth and not spouse. Usually ends with spousal neglect, putting the baby over their relationship. Some lose love connection, short attention spans.

You have desperate love where people are thirsty for anyone to love and appreciate them, usually because of heartbreak or biological clock for love. Seeking love validation while suffering from self-doubt. Rebound love is after a break-up or divorce that stemmed from a long-term relationship. People usually rush to romance someone else to make up for hurt and emotional support, as therapy and out of spite or to hide the hurt from the outside world, including family and friends. Settled love is where people tire of the ups and downs or break-ups in previous relationships and simply settle for less or outside of their loveprint just to make it work out. They stick it out and don't try to find a matchmate. Then it's the post-marriage divorce love usually always ends in emotional scars and mental wreckage and baggage. It's damaged love and warps your perception on marriage. Most people on both parties are not open to remarry ever again.

A yearn is not to get confused for love either. Yearn is more like a craving versus love. A woman's yearn is more like a churn burning desire. A man's yearn is more like a roar of a breeding lion. This is where some people mistake affection for love.

A favorite lover is just like a favorite food, car, or song that has the certain ingredient that pleases your loveprint and flutters the heart that you cannot get enough of. That individual triggers your heart vibrations. Love of a lifetime is ideal lover, spouse category, considered soulmate, lasting connection. Soulmate love is also a spiritual connection that is supposed to match your mate's on all levels, compassion, compatibility, and loveprint being identical. A spiritual, mental, physical, and energetic connection of vibrational harmony.

Being in love is usually your inception, initial spell, a web effect passion stems from a love for something. A feeling you would love to achieve. Gratification, visions, and dreams. Then it's the spell of love which is the actual web effect because it's magical, sensational, addictive, euphoric, that triggers mid brain dopamine. It's called the web effect because it's sticky area you can get stuck, and if you do make it out of this stage and unstick yourself, you still will have been sustaining love trauma and patterns. Some people latch onto a pretend matchmate because of the past feelings they chase like a drug. It's just the addict cue from your mid brain that makes it almost impossible to get over, get out of, or give up on because of your mind's instant reward and gratification process.

A lot of people do not realize how addicted to a person's love or prototype, even lust, can be triggered in this area of web effect. You must break through this web effect or simply don't attach yourself to someone so eagerly because their web effect will spill over with you to the next relationship. It's very tricky, and you have to be aware of it or people that master the art of the web effect and play on it using it as manipulation for motives to dupe your heart for sex or pure inner and exterior advantages. This is a very hazardous part of love and a level that needs to be analyzed and secure once you find out what really love is and means to you and discover your own unique loveprint, path, and identity. This also is why it plays a part with extrovert people not matching with introverts. Love stigmas and arousals. Most introverts match better with other introverts because they are truly similar.

Most of us are not doing the rituals and routines to make us love great. You will never love at the true quality on the outside if not on your inside first within. Your heart is full of love and vibrational contagious energy you attract inward and outward. It's not that you cannot only let someone else in to dictate, abuse, and crush your heart, it is also self-sabotaging. You are your own person and worst critic. Don't let yourself deter you from your lovepath and print. Self-infliction is from your own core and your ego is the voice of your fears. Must self-engage with reality, not mysticism; it's cosmetology and science. Work on your neurobiology and start to architect the love and person you desire to become that is your true self-identity in you. The heart is battle-proof and will triumph your mind anytime.

Remember what triggers nerve impulse: a physical and chemical change that moves along a process of a neuron after stimulation and carries a record of sensation or an instruction to act. These are all levels of love you must know and beware of to prevent nervous breakdowns, stress, and anxiety.

- Chapter 7 -

"Love Is an Action"

Love is not just saying, "I do!" It is something you go through and make it through. Perpetual love. Real love is an action and ongoing. What you put into love is what you get out and plays a huge part. It's love concoctions, formulating, and reciprocated love that are strong elements and key role-playing factors for that strong continuous longevity. The loving vibration connection should be magical and couples' goal to maintain and contribute alignment and being entuned to each other's loveprint. Focus should be on your partner after you learn to love yourself and master yourself and emotions, actions. It will enhance practice for lifemates.

Honesty is another important aspect of love and an action to it. Even if it means hurting your mate to help them grow and keep the communication strong and open. Or it would not be accountability in you guys' love. Accountability is a policy with honesty, and you have to hold yourself and partner to be accountable to the love and relationship shared. Especially to stay on love's true course.

For example, I did a recent poll online on my social media feed and asked a question for people to answer honestly and to be open.

"If I could only give you a rose small enough to fit in the size of a teardrop bottle for a vase because of my tight situation, would you still love me and appreciate it? Honestly!

"Or would you lie, scared to hurt my feelings, and not bring it inside your workplace beside your coworkers that just got a dozen roses of edible fruits dipped in chocolate?"

You reading this book can answer this, too, yourself. Of course the poll showing the tiny rose in a teardrop bottle caption was in awe, but it was also laughed at, or the majority of people saying "of course" or "yesss!" You have to consider the mockery and laughter as a hell no! And not people being completely honest. This is the same type of dishonesty we suffer from in our love or building relationship all because people want to protect their partners' feelings and ego. You cannot feed into others' ego and must be sincere and pure-hearted all the way around your vibrant sphere to maintain your loving chemistry, too.

We also cannot see people's brainwaves or see people's mind frame. You can read facial expressions and body language that's suggestive, but this also can be misleading or misunderstood. Remember, an innocent face hides more than a lying tongue. It is like 2 guitarist/pianist instruments need to be tuned first, then they can both play together in harmony. That's what honesty, accountability, and integrity gets you in the action of love. Making your bond very strong and establishing an honest foundation from the very beginning stages of your love to ferment.

Next I want to tackle one of the most cliché actions of love that the world's perception of it is technically illogical, which is the ultimate 50/50 rule, meaning what I do for you, you've got to do the same exact for me. Most people believe this is obligatory and mandatory. An essence of their marriage or relationship. I think it should be absolutely obliterated from people's logic and relationships.

People honestly feel like whatever they put into the relationship, give, show, etc., they are supposed to get back equally from their partner. Most mistake getting taken advantage of in the relationship and use the 50/50 rule as a safety device like a put option in the stock market, where if your stocks go low, it will cash out before they crash and you lose money.

I call it tit-for-tat. It's no keeping score and track record of all your good deeds, time, money, and love versus your partner. Whereas, a lot of marriages and relationships have been dissolved because of money and financial issues stemming from the 50/50 rule.

To realize the problematic cause of that bizarre rule is to recognize that real love is priceless and you cannot expect nobody to match your efforts. You are meant to do things from the kindness of your heart and from the heart, out of pure love. Especially if you truly love them.

The 50/50 rule puts a stipulation on your love and a strain on any relationship building or developmental stages. Not saying for you to be too kind to where people take your kindness for weakness. What if you give but your partner cannot match that because of their condition, means, or situation? Do you love them any less? Be honest with yourself and ask, "Am I being selfish and expecting too much in return instead of loving wholeheartedly?" What you must understand and learn is to relax, let go, and trust in your love and your heart. Mainly because it all balances itself out. Like it's going to be times when you can give your all, then it will be times where you can only give a little or absolutely nothing at all. And vice versa with your loved one. However, please just don't keep score with that tit-for-tat syndrome. It's not a game or a competition. You see so many ruined relationships over people that's steadfast on this 50/50 action, using it as an open mission statement to their loving relationship. How can you truly love and give your all if you're too busy keeping tallies? It's simply a waste of time, and please trust in the process that it will all equal out eventually.

Love is still the most awkwardest verb known with all its ups and downs, headaches, and heartbreaks. Even though it's an elite supreme emotion, it always manifests into feelings and actions. The art of fulfillment. It's certain fundamental value of love. Love without fulfillment is ultimate failure. Even if you have no certain idea how to solve it or get there, still push and follow your heart, then listen to it and get your results.

Learn the action of communication respectfully in a relationship. If you give away your power and saying affirmations that you cannot find love, you're brainwashing and hypnotizing yourself. This is what they call self-loathing versus self-loving. Self-sabotage on your subconscious to continuously feed your ego's fear and doubt, which leads further to depression and signs of anxiety.

When we wake up, our willpower and energy is the strongest. People are addicted to distraction with digital dementia. Transformation helps you get your creativity, love, energy, and light back in you. Most of us use and function in a beta wave brain, from beta to alpha. Your virtual reality of love you turn into your head to reality. Love must be an unconditional action.

Some more actions of love are first getting to know and learn a person. Respecting a person. Matching a person. Does your personal space and perspective match or possibly your loveprint? Selfless, unselfish, loyal, and benevolent concern and love. Additions, positive energy, all plus signs and positivity. Betterment, a better you and better them. Compromise and compassion. Trust, equality, you know the truth from the first sound, look, and inner harmony bell vibrations. Couple goals, projects, exercise, etc. Intimacy, perpetual intimacy of different kinds, not just sexual. Forgiveness and understanding to let go and move forward without holding grudges.

Love action is not just to feel passion, devotion, tenderness for, or to take pleasure in. Love action is dedication, inspiration, and perpetual progress and growth.

Some people growing up were not taught how to love from their parents. Some parents actually show tough love and don't hug their children or say the love directly, which doesn't mean they do not love their children, they just don't show the action of love. So how can you express your love if you were never shown love? The answer lies in your heart. All of us are born with human nature, including instinct, survival skill sets, and love. Love is not adoptive, it is in you. Some people may have a troubleshoot area expressing it. Your heart is the target area to pull all your love from once you understand how to shift and shape it to push your love outward effectively to be reciprocated.

The science of human beings including social, environment, relations, and culture is all an action based on love. One out of 10 people is depressed and suffers from lovelorn. Everyone looks for a platform in love to stand on or base off of. Your heart is a platform and base of the love you need within you.

Remember, the worst type lie is to yourself and not having your own love identity or interlock with your loveprint. Pablo Picasso says whatever you can imagine is real. You must dismantle this delusion of someone else's fictitious love story as your own. Rewrite your own love story. Don't be forced to other love stigmas. Must purge your heart of impurity. Your self-made love versus someone else's print needs to be number one priority to focus on and detach from. Move beyond mindless consumption of love and build love and longevity. Now people look for framework to fit their patterns and behavior of love for optimizing.

The first heartbreak from childhood usually is once you find out that Santa Claus is not real. Once you discover this, your perception of reality bends and your heart may even harden a little. It is the same way once you are conscious of your loveprint and that it actually exists. Except your heart will thrive in vibration harmony versus heartache.

It was a recent survey that says it's a shortage of economically attractive men. Your love action should not be based on status. Nor looking for someone with a certain status. Love is not control. You're not supposed to have controlled love. People hate being controlled or in controlled love relationships or marriages, which always lead to break-ups and divorces. Some people simply don't know they're being controlling or too timid to let their partner know they are too controlling.

People must learn to be able to have real conversations to clarify and be specific to their partner. It needs to be clarity in any love for it to exist in harmony. They do not know about your heart's desire, what you want, or what you dislike unless you communicate clearly to them so they can correct whatever is offensive to you.

You must collaborate and understand people to grow. You also need to be patient and lots of clarity being in love. People have so much distraction with so little time that they fail at communicating the right way. Their intent may come across different from their actions, emotions, and what they really mean. It's hard for others to understand you when you don't state yourself clearly.

Focus on trust, connection, and truth as your love action and you will make it through the dip hardship of love and relationship building. Some people honestly think they're always doomed to fail with love. However, they do not take the proper love actions and process.

- Chapter 8 -

"Friendship/Loveship"

Some of the most beautiful love stories since the beginning of time were built on friendship. You can eventually fall for one of your friends, business partners, trainer, etc., from daily routines, sharing compassion, ample time together, and created chemistry. Most friends know you, the real you and everything you go through or been through. Highs and lows, even every single emotional episode you go through, too.

A lot of people think their close friends should stay in the "friend department," not crossing over to the lover intimacy lane. The difference between lovers and friends is you need to be friends to function at a lover peak of success and longevity. Most lovers have started out as close friends, and the study ratio shows they are 76 percent more likely to stay married than couples that were not friends first. However, I am not implying looking for love in only your friends. I am simply suggesting that you establish a friendship with your lover first, not just a mere bond.

Stop trying to find the key to their heart, and find the key to unlock your own heart, and open it up to be loved by one that you establish and build a solid friendship with. You cannot have a true loveship without having a friendship first. This is why a lot of people jump head-first into relationships. It crashes and burns out even faster. It's common repeated mistakes and patterns we too often make blinded.

Even with all the lovers and friends stigmas that people frown at, that dissolves but the love doesn't die as one might suspect. It still lingers to this very day and often is unrequited, depending on time of year, or season, and which one of them is feeling. Usually after a break-up or hard time, they always have a friend they can go to and vent or be intimate with. Not as of an emotional distress rebound, but only because of their friendship and understanding they have built over time since day one.

Interesting people let you talk to show you how interesting you truly are. Listening versus talking. This is what most friendships are based on, respecting, intake, being there to listen, and share valid communications.

Some people overanalyze and rationalize. Friends look past people's words even if they speak like it's fine and okay. Consider friendships and people's feelings. They will be more open and share their feelings.

People also have lack of knowledge, not the lack of love. They don't know the verbatim details. If you want closeness, not desired intimacy, you should also establish a solid friendship with your partner. Know your role in the friendship and relationship. Being specific and clarity is important, so you need to express them for people to act.

When people fear friendship/loveship, they need to simply learn about rock-solid foundation versus windy foundation being established, which every relationship is established off some type of foundation, sexual included. Friendships lead to super vulnerability, and people are very afraid of that. It fears people from years of bondage, and frees it to heal from previous relationships' trauma, emotional distress, and hurtful anxiety drag.

Once you put your focus on something like facing your friendship fear and thinking your love doesn't necessarily need an established friendship-based foundation, you can deal with it and begin to incorporate in your relationship. Establish becoming better friends with your mate, wife, and as a couple. When you hear someone refer to their spouse or lover as their best friend, the energy is felt with emphasis. Even though they did not say best friend in actual emphasis, it's still felt. You may even hear or read comments calling the couple lovebirds or tangible love words. Whereas friendship is an actual pillar of love.

When it comes to you so easily, you won't respect it because no value from it. You fake it and eventually the real feelings manifest directly on your relationship. It could even be indirectly sought.

People use emotional weakness to control, or domination, manipulation, and intimidation. Femme fatales' method such as beauty as a tool. Also emotional pressure, subtle persuasion. She can't live with people she can't control. Will try to steal your vision and desire unreasonably until you resign. It is not just femme fatale seduction, it's all seducers that have the art of seduction down to attempt or mislead you. However, you typically can prevent these types of tactics by establishing a friendship with someone prior. You will see their patterns and learn their parallel behaviors. Then could avoid them without opting your time or heart on the line.

Psychologic techniques used to push people in compliance to a certain pattern. We need to break these patterns. We are not patterns, we're people. You create a story without friendship and create the fiction for the person. It could take months to lead up to that one desired, valued, specific, or drastic movement. You can't put someone through psychologic test to tailor them into your reason or suggestionable path to step into or experience. They can come into your world and grounds without using misleading tactics, or you can shape a friendship solid and move theirs. If people suggest you have an agenda, it gives them an idea you're not trying to be a friend or establish a friendship. You must strip anxiety, fear, and being nervous to establish a loving friendship or cross over into the love lane of a preexisting friendship established.

Friendships are so important and pivotal to open up dialogue. It is good to engage being a better friend and person with love from the heart. The main fears from friendship is failure, success, or judgements. A real love periodic table evolves with friendship and takes time for the checklist to your heart.

For people that cannot feel empathy or love, they can learn how through friendships also because a friend helps you heal, vent, and let go of hurt. Adding true value to you and your life with the connection of love and trust to help peel layers of encrusted distortion narratives. A friend can inspire you and understand you better along with being trustworthy. The Bible also says the benefit of a friend and the bliss.

It was a viral clip from Facebook of 2 toddlers that were friends in NYC that ran up to hug each other, excited and overwhelmed, like it had been years since they last saw each other. In fact, it was actually only 2 whole days. The father wrote we need more unconditional love like this in the world. The boys said my friend was excited and overwhelmed with joy. One was black and the other friend was white, both 2 years of age. They didn't see color barrier or divide prisms, they saw with their heart and vibrations for the unconditional love aligned. These biases and prejudices we develop are simply influenced by the world practice or passed down through generations. Babies are not born with hate or prejudice.

This is a prime example that goes hand-to-hand with friendship and love. People lose senses of their real heart vibrations and loveprint and take on the distortion of reality with an illusion of someone else's love perception versus their own once again. We're all hardwired into a sense of the world through storytelling and visual pictures and sound. We must rewire our mind frame, be open to true friendship without being timid or too introverted to make solid connections in the vibrations of open space. It is a divine narrative in us all. Please don't reinterpret everything into a negative. Most people take friendship for granted and do not know it. A true friend is not just a blessing, it could be blocking a blessing from your life matchmate that has the same matching biorhythm of your loveprint sensationally. Not just kids, all of us are born with a natural path and print to our inner vibration. However, we're so disconnected nowadays and picked up people's poison, behavior patterns, ideologies that we adopt as our own. Detached, we must regain the entrance to our heart and loving foundation where the seat of your very spirit sits divine, wholeheartedly pure and sincere.

You must go beyond mind over matter. It should only be heartfelt is the only thing that matters. Remember, your mind will trick you because of the ego's fear that it pushes into your subconscious to play out and alter your heart vibrations and command desires. Also remember not even going with your gut feelings because it will deceive you, as well. Some believe the gut/stomach is the second brain of the body and your gut/stomach signals your brain.

Next I want you to also look at friendship as a pre-relationship. To be a great friend, you have to be open, selfless, a listener, honest, gratification/appreciation, and reciprocal. If your friendships don't last, than the odds are neither will your actual relationships and chance at true romance. You need to recognize this is a fact and the focal point begins within you, and the breakdown in the previous chapters shows you valid solutions and how to problem-solve troubleshoot areas from your emotions, past traumas, and psychological driven influences. Some even adopt from their parents or antisocial habits from digital medium world they are boxed inside. You must live outside your phone to make friends and have success connecting friendships and loveships. Remember, loveships are relationships built off friendships and one of the strongest elements and foundation pillars of true love, not lust.

How do you make a friend or friends if you're an introvert? You must go out and mingle. Get off social sites, unless it's a group event to have people engage in whatever fields or preference areas you like. Even if it's a small niche target area you love or feel you want to grow more and explore that new lane.

In life we must learn to switch our focus from negative to positive as it consumes our mental or physical. Three happy habits. Change the way you act in circumstances that arrive. Make a constant control at all your adversity, challenges and obstacles. We can stop them only how we see them and respond to the adversity. The more you condition your mind for success and the best, it will program into reality and become. It's just like if a computer is badly programmed, it will spit out bad output, info, data, and errors. Also remember after 21 days, everything can become a habit, including people, so attach to great friendships.

We all are so used to that same door, that once it's shut and locked, we continue to twist, pull, wiggle, and bang or kick on it to get back in. However, if we simply relax, take a deep breath, and look around, turn around and you will see all types of doors... yellow doors, blue, green, gold, white, and pink to open.

- Chapter 9 -

"Matchmate"

A matchmate is not finding a match online or a dating app. Neither is it matching profiles, likes, ideals, or characteristic traits. Nor matching prototypes like a memory card game.

A matchmate is someone that your loveprint matches with and all aspects. A direct connection and direct contact to your loveprint. Some people believe you're only entitled to one in your whole lifetime, so this cliché is another soulmate stigma. It's nothing wrong with believing in soulmates; however, I just think people are confused between having a spiritual connection with someone versus the same soul as someone else. No two people have the same soul or heart. You can have the same matching heart rhythm and vibrations. You cannot hack no one's heart or have a data spreadsheet of it and see their heart algorithm and secrets.

In this chapter I will show you how to be open to discover your actual matchmate decreed by your heart's loveprint. Also key learning strategies to put you on your matching path and to summon your true matchmate with vibration energy attractions.

I want to first open up this further dialogue on an actual matchmate. First you need to change your matching concepts, social norms, and patterns already induced in your head or perceptions. Then renew with a straightforward realistic potential matchmate that your heart yearns and craves in harmony for to flutter together.

This example I will use socks. You would not wear a blue sock with a red sock, right? Unless you were colorblind and couldn't differentiate. Or you wouldn't wear a polka-dot sock with a plaid sock because they do not match. Same reasons people do not wear an ankle sock with a tube sock or a church sock with a legging. Even if they're the same matching color, they're still not a match in dimensions. You rarely see adults with one sock on and one sock off because that's taboo and a big no-no. However, you will see plenty of kids dressed for the day with one sock on and one sock off because they do not have no interlock concepts of matching stigmas or prisms. They don't have society influences, perceptional filters, or a periodic table of matching. They match whatever vibration they generate from their heart naturally. It may be funny to us or odd, but to them it's absolutely right and correct match, heartfelt.

These are the same matching cycles and narrative patterns we are stuck into that blocks and alienates us from our true potential matchmate. A lot of people don't realize what they're doing wrong and usually blame others for not being their ideal type or for their actions, which usually is either not enough attention, being attentive, or neglect. However, it is not them or their fault, it is you and your fault because of the same standard profile patterns you possess and are blind to see and let go of. A lot of people make mistakes for their ex or first mate/lover as a standard for all matches and for their next matchmate to have those same qualities and loving matching traits, which this is hazardous because you get stuck in the ideal dream match state of mind that's unrealistic with your ideal prototype and the ample standard stipulations you require from them. It's a build process to start within you first to project out to be reciprocated. Again you must spot and identify if you're self-sabotaging and have these same troubleshoot areas. Remember, what looks good to you always is not necessarily good for you. Especially if someone fits you and looks suitable to sustain your companionship and checklist. You should only have and follow the checklist of your heart. This is why people have a loss connection versus a love connection or a true chance for a matchmate romance of a lifetime.

However, it's not hard to find your matchmate if it's what your heart is looking for versus what your head is looking for. We love or like things that are bad or unhealthy for us around the clock with no filters or regards. If you align your open heart wholeheartedly with divine path of your loveprint, you will find a matchmate with a direct connection, compatibility, same loving chemistry, and once close enough, you can hear your heartbeat in sync to the same biorhythm as them sensationally by being in tune.

People always say you are so worthy of love, but it is already in you. You just have to work on bringing it out. The future is there to be created full of love from you and others. It is not a formula or scientific. It's all within you and matching your heart first. People need to be able to embody it, imply it, and intake mentally. The greatest people are self-managed. Get your vision goal and empower yourself to thrive in your troubleshoot areas, pattern that's habitual to break by daily progress and intercession.

People lose their wonder from childhood, rely on matchmakers and referrals from friends or coworkers, and don't go beyond wonder to curiosity and explore earthly options first nature of their true love circumference. They continue to box themselves in the augmented reality of the world.

Mastering open communication skills and landing your communication directly, respectfully, and honestly. What matters is what people hear. What we evoke to others and what we actually do. Argue like you're right, but listen like you're wrong. Most people want to be in a relationship just to see what they can get out of it. Not to find a potential matchmate, directly or indirectly. Most people believe if it is meant to be, then it will. I think this is another fabricated cliché. You can learn from trial and error or from someone else's trial and error. Also, we have freedom of choice and free will. Most just sucked into society cycles of sandstorms and loses consciousness or simply take for granted educating themselves. Predictable outcomes help. You made a bad choice and built up pain, resentment, and regret from dating that person or marrying that person you deluded as ideal matchmate. It is hard teaching people over 25 unless trauma in their life. Leverage crisis with adversary growth. You use adversity and turn conditions, state of mind frame, and emotions from negative to positivity. Disrupt proximity, then disassociate yourself from old prototypes to people of your matchmate vibrations from the melody of your heart.

Matchmate is not just an awe in a person. Some people's charm is only held to arouse sexual passion. Not every charm is charming and can also have hidden agendas, and this is a lot of people's fears, too. Vulnerability hurts us and leaves us open to be hurt and preyed on. To become tough, you have to let go of the weak links inside of you or your fearing ego. All hearts are good and pure, some just broken and frozen or became cold along with mind being bitter with emotional distress. It only exists because of their past hurting relationship or being crushed, heart shattered from a matchmate from childhood that could not possibly co-exist abnormally.

You're supposed to build self-confidence. People don't act on finding a true matchmate or love, they simply sit back, timid and playing on their insecurities. They go to Starbucks, sit in a loveseat expecting to connect with an ideal matchmate secluded. You need to have open space with baby steps to boost confidence and speak to people with full-on engagements. Mingle. It could be a future friend, business partner, or spouse. You never know. It doesn't necessarily have to be a matchmate. Your correct matchmate to define the vibrations of your heart takes time and practice. You can't rush it. The season will come, it is a season and time for everything. However, in that germination process, you can be using that time to work on you, loving you, perfecting you, and projecting your inner love externally versus using time to lie dormant like a bump on an old log.

We're isolated, and in everything, we box ourselves in. Including our box phone. It's a metaphor. We go from a box room to a box car or Uber, then to a box cubicle or workplace. Then, when you die, you go straight into a box coffin. We need to get out into open space and off mobile devices to mingle and reflect the radiant loving energy. Make people feel your love and the Earth vibrate like an earthquake from it. Your love from your heart is so strong and contagious with its gravitational pull that you could make it rain with radiant love attraction cues all around. That's that non-sexual glow people tap into. Do not recycle same love and romance from past or prior experience.

How can you truly have lived life without ever generating the energy and electricity of your loveprint and that friendship/relationship to find your God-given matchmate? You find your loveprint, then get clear on it, always act on your vision and discovery. Most people are asleep to their loveprint and lose their heart feelings and sense, they rely on gut instincts and automated subconscious or alter fear of the ego.

We are all interconnected, something can empower you or influence you. Especially with loving people. Love is the law of the land, highly contagious. Some people you see stand out in a crowd, and you can see their magic and true love radiantly glowing, and their gravity of love consuming and engulfed in a sphere all around them. The aura of the heart chakra is evident in them that a blind man can feel it with his enhanced other senses. Some may be able to even taste or smell the love. They have a natural love and committed to discover more ways to keep love ongoing with perpetual reciprocation. It is miracles and wonders in loveprints. This is where some of the most greatest love stories were created from and the premise of love's baseline from the heart. Please don't settle, keep on your path to your loveprint and find your matchmate. A lot of us are simply lost of past pain. You must use all the strategies and solutions stated in previous chapters to reprogram your brain, because we won't let pain or accept it. Do not allow people's opinions to move your life or social norms influence or alter it. Everything else is secondary from that point.

Make people want to follow you and inspire them with love. Love is the only tool you need for longevity on this Earth, at home, or school and workplace. Understand human nature and their value and create a loving cause. Then watch how it is matched or mastered or simply practice. Play into their psychology with love, appealing to things to motivate them. Inclusive is a great leader trait.

Are you enrolling people in your life just to see how you see it? Are you more interested in your own self, thoughts, and ideas versus others? Ask yourself. So this means you cannot be a better listener. Think about people as characters in a movie. Are you motivated to learn them, see what makes them tick, and the cause, effect, and triumph role they play? Or only interested in casting self in own love story? Try to learn something new about them, their childhood, or devastating out of them. It all helps you be more selfless and not selfish. Love is all about being selfless. Helps prepare for matchmate.

We are masters at reading people's body language, from postures to facial expressions. Maybe we don't have our body language in check and have an emotional, uptight, or provocative body language for potential matchmates, not realizing the first impression body language statement we're stamping and stinking up all over the place. For example, if you have a slouch posture, you can be perceived as lazy or be signaling a leave-me-alone emotional warning or simply anger. Anger is an intoxicating emotion. When you talk angry, you can feel the real intensity in it, so imagine your body language during this stage. It will run off any person. If you read body language and sit in silence, one topic/subject you mention will spark their interest and to engage fully in warming conversation and elevated convos. If you treat people as they're smart, they will do well because they're believing it. It's a placebo effect. It is a very competitive world, so you go inward versus outward, being discouraged. You must break it and reverse that.

How to differentiate between a fake smile and a genuine smile? You look into their eyes and facial expression. Emotional expressions are learned behavior and are universal. Facial expressions, both blind and regular athletes have the same facial expressions of emotions if they win or lose. All expressions like anger, fear, surprise, sadness, happiness, excitement, shame, disapproval, lustful, envious and contempt can all be read and perceived right or wrong way. Maybe even offensive, but most people are not aware of it and affect sensory organs. You can recognize your matchmate if you pay more attention to facial features, expression, and body language could approve life. Even your hormones and neurotransmitters in your brain play a role in your certain facial expressions, not just during sex. The pineal gland is connected body through mind. If I think, therefore I am! The world is made out of physical and non-physical stuff. Interactionism is mind and bodies interact with each other. If you convince mind and body to do something, it will and manifest one way or other or in variables. Premises assume that so your emotions turn into feelings and manifest to influence your facial expression and body language. This is why people say don't wear your feelings on your sleeve or your heart on your sleeve. You may deny your emotions or your distress and dismay like you're having a great day. However, people and your parents or someone close to you can read you like a book and so clearly like you are transparent.

Affecting people in proper mood, this is how you influence and persuade people. We're vulnerable to the moods and attitudes of people. Our moods are extremely contagious moods, and energy influences better than words. You can alter people by the moods, too. The level of seduction, the way you approach them and mood. A relaxed and calm mood makes a woman feel safe and more loving and an irresistible attraction to you. Relaxed and undefensive about it. You can defuse it or anything with a calming, loving approach and mood. Most people don't know their passion or how to find it or influence their mood. A mental belief is different from illusion of a trick. You must be able to switch your moods from negative to positive before they reflect outwards, which your potential matchmate can see and detect, then do an about-face military 180-degree straight turnaround. You want your matchmate to feel welcome in your vibrant space of warm thriving love to be able to connect directly and grow in harmony as one, where both your spirits touch. You want them to run right to you, not away from you.

Everyone has triggers, and good and bad triggers. Some emotional, some life-altering leading to drastic changes. We all have primates and animal nature and loving instincts in us. Remember the law of aimlessness. Figure out what your matchmate is really supposed to do in your life and coming in it. Everybody is differently brain-wired, structure, etc. If you do what everyone is doing to find matchmates, you will be like everyone else with same results, disappointments of high ratio break-ups and divorce rates. Find your special niche, loveprint, passion, and you will find your matchmate. That voice telling you who you are, what to do, and what's next. Master primary in collections, and listen to yourself and heart. You'll find primal attraction matchmate.

- Chapter 10 -

"Love Prevails All"

Love prevails, likes fail. Love conquers all, no mistaking, and makes the world and households go around. Do not mistake likes for love. Most of your social media likes were just mere gestures of support, love, engagement, or a social response interaction on a trendy wave or hot topic that people are in a frenzy over. It is simply computer love in a digital world and not authentic love. It is not tangible to your heart and soul.

Love truly outweighs any probative effect, emotional or obstacle. Love outweighs it all. Love overrules hate. Hate in the world is simply created by people's influence and ego. Hate is really, a fear turned into a progressive emotion, then manifest into a feeling with usually a plan of action. Usually people that hate are inferior because their hearts are locked and non-responsive. They do not know how to clear the clutter in their head and restore the divine path to their true pure hearts. Love trumps everything, including fear, hate, distress and conditions. Even if it's your fitness you feel weighs you down because it's not your ideal physical appearance, and you hate your blemishes that only you care about and dwell on versus loving and appreciating yourself. You will naturally elevate those outward insecurities and navigate your loving confidence. Remember the solutions you have read in this book. Let go of hurt and pain, clear it out by addressing it. Go back and confess it, then do your daily affirmations and rituals as routine step-by-step. Don't compare to past, contrast with stipulations, hinder your love in a box. Then you can love wholeheartedly from the heart chambers.

In this final chapter I will further teach you how to create the self-value of love and how to focus on your vibrations and aura without rushing romance. I will review some strategies and solutions from previous chapters as well. Before we get back into how to love, I wanted to share with the readers my method of teaching effectively to people that have past trauma, emotional distress, psychological dilemmas, society perceptional influences, and suffering from constant break-ups. Sincere and pure intentions of love from my heart. Certain things such as solutions, methods, awareness, and formulating are reiterated in various forms to help you recognize and reimply it. This tactic creates reassurance for your mental to turn it into a reality of actions and willpower. By helping your brain pick up patterns, it will help you to practice them, too. You also start to learn and understand a lot clearly, and often answer any question or loose open ends. What I do when I do not understand a problem or concept, I reread it. I encourage you to go back chapter to read back, or I'd suggest you read the book over to help you intake and develop better. This book is meant to decree love and share your love once you clear the clutters of your head and heal your heart with a bandage of love.

Okay, back on subject. What is your love status? Open, honest, selfless? You must possess the key traits and elements of love. Also have the concoctions of love, both connection and chemistry. Then commitment and communication clearly and respectfully. True love is not hard to find. It is like a revolving door, it keeps going and going or keeps coming around and around. It is never truly a shortage of love, especially long as it's humans on this planet. Love is law and our true nature. It is up to you to love or let go and try elsewhere. Some love cannot be fixed once broken. Others can be fixed and stabilized or salvaged, if both parties put in 110 percent effort.

Trust in the process, bring out your heart. Do not feed the machine and lapse back into the same pattern behaviors and wrong choices of people and love. You know better now. If you really want a change in your life, you have to have a change in heart or a cleanse of the heart to replenish.

Again I will sum up overall focal points, keys, strategies, and how-to solutions for the whole book in a brief whole.

Once you are awake/aware of you being in someone else's love shadow, like the matrix effect, you become conscious and reverse-engineer it, not programmed.

It is a blockage to the path of your true heart and love, must remove blockage to the path and unveil your divine loveprint.

How you want to be loved is how you should love others. You can be loved, love, and find love. Remember how to love. You must first recognize all the filtered love traits and habits you picked up or ideology of people, movies, visuals, etc., that love template bestowed in you from parents and generations. Then you need to reprogram your subconscious with affirmations of your heartfelt vibrations after you recognize it actually exists, and the love you've been feeling was scripted into your perceptions, which is why you cannot get love right because it's someone else's vain desires of love and don't match your actual loveprint decree. Then find your true loveprint that will never lead you astray. Soul search in depth and become tuned into your heart's desire. It will not mislead you or deceive like your mind and ego will. Make a direct connection, establish a friendship/loveship with honest and respectful open communication, commitment, and discover your matchmate.

Now I want to elaborate and touch on your chakras and the human aura. Science has verified its existence, like a disease can be detected before it actually surfaces physically in the body. This human aura is within us all, and this energy field originates within and glows and shines once your chakras is aligned through the colors. It influences human behavior, relationships, love, and success. Through mantras and daily meditations you can develop certain abilities to be strong and control circumstances, influence your moods and life. Your chakras or energy forces within.

Science of the spoken word you can actually direct the accelerating of your spirit aura into the accumulation of the subconscious electronic belt. You can feel the renew thought process and feeling liberating the aura within you, which governs the flow of light and patterns.

It is said once you have the mastery of the base chakra, you attain the omnipresent consciousness and self-mastery of the base of the spine chakra.

The solar plexus chakra is the center of feeling where you employ the energy of emotion. Usually generated by the sun energy in motion to realize God's consciousness using the full potential of the desire body, you have full momentum of water molded in a matrix of love. Through spoken words, a wave of light goes across the Earth, leading atoms and electrons to come into pure alignment.

The crown chakra is where consciousness and true wisdom is known and goal of self-mastery of time and space. The firing of the crown with wisdom creates a magnet that draws the energies up from the base of the spine up through each of the successive chakras, which are the centers of our God-awareness and the enlightenment and experience of knowing all things without being taught or forced. Our awareness.

The third eye chakra you return to the consciousness of absolute good through the third eye chakra. Vibrating in the emerald green of the science of truth gives you the immaculate picture of individuals, love of civilizations, and of the divine patterns.

You can always tell whether or not you are looking through the third eye or through the two eyes. The third eye always gives you the immaculate concept of the blueprint of life as well as the discrimination to know good and evil. The two eyes give you a relative and often unclear perception and perspective on life. They do not penetrate beyond the physical plane unless in an exalted vision, the faculty of sight be accelerated by miraculous intercession.

Through the all-seeing eye of God, the inner eye of the soul, you tune in to what should be in reality, instead of what may be occurring in the actualities of the present (Matt. 6:22).

"The light of the body is the eye." —Jesus Christ

The throat chakra, the power in man and woman which represents the power of precipitation. The word becoming flesh, spirit becoming tangible in matter. The shortening of the days or cycles of karma occurs through the correct use of your spoken words.

When you speak, "I am loved—I love myself before I can love anybody else," and follow it with affirmations of light, we begin the transmutation process. Freeing up your mind, self-doubts, and heartaches. Anything and everything that proceeds from the throat chakra coalesces in form, for good or for ill, by the action of the power of the spoken words. Its scientific use is the truth that shall make you free when you apply it diligently every day.

Say these affirmations daily: "I am the light of the heart shining in the darkness of being. I am projecting my love out into the world to erase all errors and break down all barriers. I am the power of infinite love, amplifying itself until it is victorious world without ending!"

Remember, be not overcome with hate, but overcome hatred with love.

The heart chakra is the most important chakra. The energy from it is distributed to the other 6 major chakras and to the 5 minor chakras of the secret rays. Also to all the cells and nerve centers. The heart is where the pink fires of love burn brightly.

When you keep the heart in the vibration of love in compassion for all life, you discover all regard for life as one. Within the heart are the issues of all life that leads to one source.

The magnet that you create within the heart chakra is the ascending triangle. The more you meditate upon this triangle superimposed upon the heart chakra, the more it becomes the reality of the dimensions of the sacred Trinity, embodied in the threefold flame sealed in the hidden chamber of the heart.

If it calls, it compels the answer, so the presence of this force field of this triangle combined with the letters "I AM LOVED—I LOVE MYSELF" of the heart flame will draw the descending triangle of consciousness into the heart chakra. Also the merging of the Creator and creation through the intercession of consciousness. Self is the foundation of our exercise whereby the aura of man/woman becomes the aura of the Creator.

The hidden chamber of the heart, your threefold flame of life is sealed in the 8petaled chakra called the hidden, or secret, chamber of your heart. The threefold flame, or divine spark, makes your heart a replica of the Creator's heart.

It is literally a spark of sacred fire from God's own heart. Also the threefold flame is your soul's point of contact with the supreme source of all life and love. It's really your true potential to become the fullness of all that your real self is.

It embodies 3 primary attributes from the plumes: the Creator's power, wisdom, and love. By accessing the power, wisdom, and love of the Creator anchored in your threefold flame, you can fulfill your love and reasons for being.

The threefold flame, your heart is indeed one of the best gifts of the Creator. Within it there is a central chamber surrounded by a forcefield of such light and protection that we call it a cosmic interval. It is a chamber separated from matter, and no probing could ever discover it. It occupies simultaneously not only the third and fourth dimensions, but also other dimensions unknown to man/woman.

Also this central chamber, called the altar of the heart, is the connecting point of the mighty silver cord of light that descends from your God presence to sustain the beating of your physical heart, giving you life, purpose, and cosmic integration.

I encourage all of you to appreciate, love, and treasure this point of contact that they have with life by giving conscious recognition to it. You don't need to understand by any sophisticated language or scientific postulation the how, why, and wherefore of this activity. Remember, there it burns as the true essence of love, wisdom, and power.

Each acknowledgement paid daily to the flame within your heart will amplify the power and illumination of love within your being. Each such attention will produce a new sense of dimension for you, if not outwardly apparent, then subconsciously manifest within the folds of your inner thoughts.

Do not neglect it. Draw from the Creator of the universe the power of love and amplify it within your heart. Then send it out into the world at large as the bulwark of that which shall overcome the darkness of the planet saying, "Beloved I AM! Love, wisdom, and power! Balance the threefold flame in me! I love myself from my heart outwardly." Three times. Then tell yourself you accept this manifest right here and now with full power, eternally sustained, all-powerfully active, ever expanding wholeheartedly with love. You can go online for more learned chakra research.

Remember with your daily affirmations the mirror effect, too. The power of perception will always project to your subconscious, then into a reality automated already. Therefore, by you using the mirror to look at yourself to further assist your affirmations, it helps your visuals and solidify whatever you're speaking into change and existence. The same way how you looking in the mirror creates self-doubt by giving negative acknowledgement to your psyche thinking you look fat or ugly. Then you start to feel and believe you really are. All this without even uttering a single word. You automated this into your head. A lot of us are guilty of it, so no need to be ashamed. Simply reverse engineer it with your manifesting rituals. This is also proof to you that affirmations actually work by the example I shared above so you recognize everything you think negative or positive is created into a feeling or an action.

The switch, what pulls you from this to that? The distractions of the world and daily routines, work, home, and your love life with people's short hyphenated attention span? Musicians encourage people to edit the story, other people's stories. It's people's ongoing perceptions.

The stories we tell ourselves and get restricted by it, start to believe in it like a magic trick. Then you tell yourself to heal that pain or part of the body. Just like you getting your adrenaline going is a pain killer, too. Be a student at life and understanding self and people. Give them a visualization.

It is losers, and it is people who learn how to love and win. Self-discipline separates people from successful people. Two types of people, one says, "I'll do it when I feel like it." The other one says, "I feel the need to love" and do it. Most people have a story to why or an excuse by the boatloads. Must unchain your mind and be conscious of not holding yourself accountable with reality.

Must make true. Alter a belief, and we change reality. A simple philosophy, fact it to you make what you take to be true on subconscious level will come to reality. Our perception what we see is what we look for. We got to break up years of beliefs and rescript years of belief on subconscious mind. Mind script that's welded into your subconscious.

Program of visual technique, bring subconscious a visual goal to bring into a reality. The old you creeps in to give you excuses not to do it, period.

Again I want you to know the love hack solutions behind this. Set up a time 5 minutes each day for your visual goal in process. Close your eyes, roll them upward, focus on your breathing, focus on your lungs and breathing exercise, put your brain in alpha state and out of a beta wave. This induces an alpha brain wave in 45 seconds. Then conjure up an image or emotional moment/events, the loving adulation. The positive emotional that will have a psychological effect if your subconscious sees it. Each person's different, some respond better to pics, forms, or words. Your senses smell it, feel it, hear it. Recreate a winning feeling, do a mental objective of that goal. Your subconscious affirms it, then act on it. When you try too hard, you choke on it. If you envision it, you create it. You must believe you deserve it. Must relieve guilt and programs inside of us from people, family, and friends. Happiness is a state of mind and a means to an end. Success and well-being, you cultivate it. You do it by being and acting with good habit.

Now let's go back to the brain and review the addiction breakdown receptors. The parallel behavior patterns in brain addiction-like responses. Brain triggers dopamine or opioids. Prefrontal cortex makes you want more, and middle is medium prefrontal cortex. Your brainwaves tell you to stop eating or doing something with a stop signal. It is triggers in the brain to help you stop certain behavior.

Like a junk food diet, it shrinks your hippocampus proteins and could cause the depression and cause mental health probably by depriving your brain. The hippocampus is the memory part of your brain. You could be healthy, non-fat, and still be unhealthy, especially with a diet deficient in cognitive. If you want your brain to function right, feed it healthy and loving things.

Huge ill health is to blame from wrong seductive love. How your brain chemistry and chemical receptors are working on love. Dopamine receptors are less response and craving sensations of reward. They're reduced between 20 to 50 percent. Everyone accepts it is a stigma when we talk about love. Also, there is no evidence that the dopamine corrects itself. You must stop the addictive ways and reward-seeking dopamine by changing your bad habit patterns into great loving habitual patterns. One day at a time, it's a life challenge for perpetual change.

We develop a template of what love means from our parents, which is wrong and not realistic, and we become in our relationship patterns and the unconscious comes, we look for things in familiar patterns again. Also people, too, so we kind of adapt to it.

How do we master our minds and life, then rewrite our mind and own love story? Set goals realistic from the previous chapters and follow through with self-accountability. Be okay with learning and experience. Accept your failures and move on, keep at your practice to master self and goals. Make it okay that life is not always going to be in your favor, going your fairy tale of a movie love story way with true love. Psychoanalyze it to become more conscious of it. Not a psychodrama that you continuously make, fuel, and play into your psychological dramatic overtones. Stop it! You really can, and I believe in you just from you choosing to read this book and taking time out to build self and finding effective solutions to help you grow and fertilize your innate love by impregnating your mind, heart, and soul with perpetual love.

It's a step-by-step, day-by-day practice model to take effect and imply them impulsive form who you are as an adult that you have stemming from childhood, past traumas, and emotional disorders.

However, you can be a little emotional for your partner, then clarify and view different. Do not make it all about you because it's gray areas to people that they don't even know or realize what they do or what is the cause of it and where it came from. You cannot control the outcome. They just need to further find themselves and space to grow in. Being good at deflecting things but not lying is key. Don't hurt their feelings but honesty hurts sometimes because the ego hides us from the truth and stinking reality we all run from, some more than others. Remember, we can't run forever and have to address that altering issue. I'm not saying entertain people's silly theatrics or playing into people's crazy. Happiness leads to good health and fitness, is key to relationship empowerment. Even outweighs the fussing, argumentative fights and reduces them totally.

Everyone crave intimacy. Sex needs to be educated, learn more about partner's sexual needs, and what sexual expectations. Sex plays a huge factor in all relationships, especially if you're in love or making physical love. Align your chakras to touch simultaneously with someone else to levitate the love of both loveprints to dance, mingle, and intertwine with each other to the same thudding harmony and biorhythm.

We have to learn to be more honest and open for sexual discussion and transparent. A person is laying the wrong foundation and afraid to ruffle feathers of lover and realness frankly. We have to be real and tender to our partner/matchmate.

The disconnect leads to infidelity. The attraction and balance is gone. Marrying the wrong matchmate for the wrong reasons can't end right. We entertain people we should not and avoid as a whole, ignoring all the red flags, cautious warning signs. You saw the sign and read it before you slipped into a false matchmate and love, then you got a crushing heartbreak and stuck with a train wreck of emotional distress that you can't seem to balance still years later and carry it on to the next potential mate, sabotaging relationship instead of building a loving foundation you're entitled to. Also if you lack self-worth, your mind needs to be right after emotional distress.

We suppress our past hurt and it snowballs, then manifests to you physically. You need to release and emotionally detox. A full release of hurt past and then you can process. Understand your perception and understand how and why people hurt.

You must find yourself, not a fake connection. Exude positive energy. People's lack of energy draws the most people the other way. It throws everything off, vibrations of love included.

A lot of people don't know their energy or chakras are off because they have blockage within and walls up, not allowing the sun to power your heart chakra because of the blocked force field you darkened yourself with and blind to. You dim your bright light within your heart of love, life, and laughter, indirectly filtering yourself, health, and loving spiritual wealth, which you block your divine blessing to give and receive love of the world and from others. The whole planet can love you from the air-wind, trees, seas, and all the animals, not just your pets. Love is not an equation, it is an action that you play a part from your heart. A give and get perpetual inevitable cycle of life.

Push forward in loving faith, not fear. When you hold on to fears and hurt, you become detached from feminine or superpower. Your life, health, peace, and worth. You heal first and let go, then rebuild after your healing process.

Most people give up after marriage vows and feel entitled. It's like once you get that dream job, you give up on working hard at it or pursuing it. Same concept in marriage. People give up and are tired of trying to love and appease each other. People get married and let go, including self. Marriage is not something you do just because of social norms and wear it around public display like a trophy. If you can't maintain yourself and gain weight or partner/ matchmate does, it needs to be addressed or set expectations from the beginning pre-marriage. People let self go and don't be honest about attraction expectations, then blame their matchmate and resent them.

The reality of what is holding us back and resentment. Appearances are highly important and play into factors problematic.

Women are not as vocal and transparent. Most people don't want to feel inadequate or love loss from fear of world views and family. People cheat for emotional and sexual issues, and honesty contributes to it, or mere curiosity from boredom. You can't always blame it on the alcohol. That alibi is too cliché throwback like a Thursday.

Some people feel like they need a lot of partners and date nights or in an open relationship because one person cannot love and please them or meet all their standard needs, which really is something deeper going on and weighing heavy on them.

We must really learn how to heal from everything first, past trauma and issues hurt you now and long run to hold on to or it. Trust me, it's possible to let go, heal, and rebuild. If you believe and practice, it's achieved.

Remember, you can create chemistry, but that amazing direct connection is being compatible to keep it lasting, not the pressure of society or because of the kids.

If a true connection really exists, then a relationship can be fixed and worked out. Again, you must understand the disconnect, and both sides make it work and willing to work. Else it's too irreconcilable and time to learn to let it go. You cannot chase or catch a diminished love like a shooting star fading into oblivion.

These develop dysfunctions, now have a child believe they can't trust love because of their perception now of love adopted from you, and you just enable the perceptional generational template of dysfunctional love. They get neglected because of their parents going through suffering, hurt, and a negative cycled relationship. So think about and be conscious of your relationship's influence of your kids or the youth. They soak everything like a sponge at all ages and very keen on observation. They can surveillance you better than an actual camera, even when you think they're not listening, looking, or sleeping.

They adopt what their parents went through and all aspects of it from divorce, abuse, hurt, drinking, drug abuse, serious domestic violence, and being in a negative unhealthy environment all to reflect on kids.

The kids need to see happy and healthy loving relationships and marriages built on real loving foundations so they have the right example to express their love and one day, too, shall find their matchmate and discover their essence of existence of their divine loveprint heartfelt. Kids have issues stem from their parents and create the problems. We normalized dysfunction, now so common in society family household, that we start to believe it's true love and human nature to behave with such non-filtered pattern habits. Just because you're in a relationship or marriage, you don't have to play punching bag on your partner or lash out just because they're there and you feel entitled. Our behavior is inexcusable, and we need to reset, reshape, and create ground rules or let go flat out, especially if it's detrimental to safety, health, or children. Maybe even for acknowledgement or showmanship having a ring and being married at a certain age and to be simply seen with a ring to be up with social norms or digital era.

The things what you dislike shows you who you are. Your uniqueness is your source of love and power. You don't need help to find the path to your loveprint. You must simply follow your heart and intuition naturally. I cannot produce it for you. My job is to show you how to clear the path blockage so you can be engaged with love and reconnect to your threefold energy within the heart and unlock the hidden chambers of your heart and unveil your love vibrations to flow outward into the world for you to attract your matchmate for a potential lifetime. He/she is out there awaiting for you to open your heart to be subjectable to drumming love with a dancing rhythm to match same as your mate. The same method approach of love that the different species on Earth tap into and dance in awe with their seducing mate.

Gather yourself and stay self-disciplined. You have to have self-awareness to make you change. Don't fall into same patterns. You must really try to see and learn your own patterns.

Remember, toxic people are bad for your health and can become cancerous. Thinking people are great and seeing them in a better light will persuade their dynamics. How to change your attitude when you persuade to change theirs, they can't feel manipulated. It needs be that they did it on their own.

Everyone tends to believe they're smart, good, etc., but those all are self-opinions. However, if someone challenges you or your belief, you will get defensive and closed off, and it may even cause fear and hatred.

The number-one thing people want is love validation from others. We're all craving that validation and seek it in pursuit of love. If you have a way to stroke their self-validation without flattery, you can persuade them to do something positive.

However, if they see through the flattery, they will see it's clear you're after something or trying to trick them, which usually they lapse back into their negativity realm. But if you hit on things that people don't hit on, see, give validation to, or don't get flattered by what everyone else flatters them about that's too obvious, you will break through, get their attention to help shift their mind to a positive. Their insecurities aren't good to flatter and interconnect. Using people's stubbornness and negative, you must go with the flow, feed their ego and talk their own language to get through to them. Same process friends and family use to connect and break through to their loved ones. However, you don't have to dumb yourself down because you will make them feel it, too. You can prove people wrong mentally and use it as positive energy and fuel to self-driven and motivation confidence within, not to hurt people that you're simply more advanced than.

Always thinking of putting yourself in a commitment to being giving, creating, and loving cosmic energy to vibrate the world. You can even use a public declaration. If you say publicly or on your social platforms, people would hold you accountable. For love affirmations, projects, actions, timeframes, etc., you simply lock yourself into your own commitment. I see a lot of social media feed with women stating this is the year or season they meet their husband. They publicly declare and push it out to the universe for it to boomerang with laws of love and gravity. So if you're waiting and reserving yourself for true love, state your facts, own it, and declare it without no pressures or anxiety behind it. It should flow naturally from the heart.

Do not live a limited life, have passion. The ones that don't want to love simply quit. Design for yourself, be enthusiastic, and build love momentum. The feeling of love is so different from the experience. Intent state of mind with which an action is done. Not habitual or excessive self-doubt. Do not intercept or interrupt the progress or course to your healing process and loveprint. Nor lack of moderation.

Your core values shouldn't. Intangible love, perpetual love. Remember your brain's thought process into feelings and emotions. Primal instinct reverse engineers we have in us all.

We dream to heal stress transmitters less. Your brain also deals with hardship, stress, anxiety, and problem solve when certain mood disorders, when you sleep. You have a natural fight-or-flee mode inside you.

We dream to solve problems, too. Your mind can create effective natural solutions and problem solving with benzo molecules. The way we understand our minds is through compartments and visuals.

Curiosity is contagious, so is love! Real love boosts your happiness, mood, and joy.

Most people want their spouse or mate to say thank you, and others want to be appreciated endlessly. Most people also don't serve to something bigger or cause it's selfless, which is the exact contrast and underlying issue.

The sweet science of love, it's not all about you...to solely love someone wholeheartedly, it is an act plural and action based on the hemisphere and aura of someone or something else without an individual agenda attached.

Master lovers are leaders and risk-takers because they're not afraid to project and share their platonic love to the world, even though it's hateful people out there that can hurt them, but they still push against all odds and have the courage to do it. Heart, love, vision, and risk-taking create loving blueprints and leaderships. Great people lifting people up and having them be part of them and invested their love in you. Look for loving friends, teams, co-workers, and influence partners all infused with creative heartfelt generated love to the world. Everything you touch shall have your vibrations and loving energy.

Your biology, a science that deals with living beings and life process, must be clear and distinct. Reconciling the loveprint path. Also your biography of love should not be a written history of someone else's life or writings. It should be your own written decree of your heart.

Finally, take the time out to a self-challenge. Write down what your definition of love is. What do you love? Who do you love? Why? What do you appreciate about them and self? What do you love most about self? What's your troubleshoot areas to fix and work on? Write down your visuals, gratifications, appreciation, etc., your loveprint, and challenge to find true loveprint design. Set a goal and time to practice daily to apply, go focus on protecting your loveprint. Try a new loving environment, people, places, books, films, music, etc.

Remember, mysticism is belief that ultimate reality is attainable through immediate intuition or insight, but it's nothing like being optimistic from the heart versus pessimistic from the head.

I want to end this book with my love to the world and all who read it and apply the love shared. Thankful to enlighten and move you from the love of my loveprint vibrations. Positive energy and blessing. I leave you with a #HowtoLoveChallenge—I challenge you to find your own loveprint!!

Epilogue

This *How to Love* book was to help you retain the value of your heart, therapy, and to retain self-value and love to project into the world, workplaces, homes, etc. Corrective thinking to transform your psychology and perceptions into your own loving contributions. Then find your loveprint.

I want all of you to value your time, too. What are you doing with your time? Are you wasting it on fruitless things you're not passionate about? Motivation. We only have a limited time on this Earth and that's a sure reality. Your time should be spent out of love and appreciation. The validation of time will show you everything. It will reveal your patterns, likes, loves, ethics. You can't get your time back or people's time back, so value it. Make your time work for you, not against you, and be cautious to what you're putting your time in that's not out of pure love from the heart. The essence of your timeline should be of passion projects and love.

* * *

Share this book or recommend it to impact or add value to a loved one who is hurting or disconnected from their path to loveprint and biorhythm.

About Author

Hitachi Choparazzi is a New York City native, by the way of Omaha, who is currently incarcerated in level 5 solitary confinement in Florence, SMU-Eyman Complex, serving an illegal sentence awaiting on Supreme Court Appeal to correct his sentence with time served. The error forces him to serve 2 years extra.

He is an entrepreneur, tattoo artist turned author. Also the sole owner of Chop-a-Style Publishing and Productions, and the owner of Chatmon Sr. Literary Agency. He has written over 20 books and including scripts to pitch to Netflix. All this while he was incarcerated to start his reform act.

Founder and CEO of Billion-Dollar Blueprint and the BDB movement/youth movement, an innovator entrepreneurship where he believes everyone has their own blueprint, like everyone has their own unique thumbprint. Based on 3 core principles—Education, Elevation, and Innovation—which he teaches the youth and people how to format and discovery key. BillionDollarBlueprintmerch.com

The face of lockdown society movement along with the voice of lockdown society movement. IncarceratedLivesMovement. com #ILM #BDB

"I do this for y'all. I love y'all, rep y'all, and believe in y'all! I won't stop giving y'all all the raw stories as God bless them in my head. I have a hundred of them up there. Anybody that has a hot hand, send me samples or any comments, suggestions to my FB, IG Hitachi Choparazzi or email: orders@chopastylepublishingllc. com Chop-A-Style Publishing LLC and Productions. TeflonLuv!"

Hitachi Choparazzi prides himself on having his own signature Chop-a-Style where he freestyles all his books. They all rhyme with innovation and original storylines. He writes prequels, sequels, trilogies, and more. Does it for the people who love to read and for all those incarcerated in state, federal B.O.P., county, and women's facilities. FB,IG,Tiktok, Twitter, YouTube-Hitachi Choparazzi

Emails: Hitachichoparazziauthor@gmail.com
Billiondollarblueprintmerch.com

Other Books and Scripts by the Author

Non-Fiction

- How to Rap; The Elementary Teaching of Hip-Hop

- How To Tattoo & Start-Up Business

- How To Digital Detox

- How To Start-Up a Food Truck Business

- How To Stop School and Mass Shootings: Dear Parents

- Incarcerated Lives Matter: The Hitachi Choparazzi Blueprint

- How to Love

- The Switch: A Social Awareness Self-Help

- Nipsey Hussle Lockdown Society Dedication—Tribute

- If Trayvon Martin Could Talk; Injustice

Fiction

- The Eagle and Weasel (1-5 series kids' book)

- She Go! (urban novel)

- Reality Show 3D-HD (urban novel)

- Hot Thots (urban novel)

- Liqz (urban novel)

- Paranormal Whisper (horror novel)

- Pimp of Da Ratchets (urban novel)

- Pimp of Da Ratchets II Vegas (urban novel)

- Pimp of Da Ratchets 3 Orange is Da New Pimp (urban novel)

- Hitachi (urban novel)

- Penitentiary Pimp (urban novel)

- Weasel Society (urban novel)

- The Big Pep and Plucker Story-She Go! Prequel (urban novel)

Screenplays/Scripts

- Top Notch

- Hot Thots

- Pimp of Da Ratchets

- Weasel Society

- Million Dollar Games–A Secret Society

- The Eagle and Weasel (animation)

Billion Dollar Blueprint is a movement we challenge and inspire you to find your individual blueprint. Our mantra is "We believe everyone has their own blueprint like everyone has their own thumbprint". With these three core principles

Education

Elevation

Innovation

Hitachi Choparazzi is the founder and CEO. Orders available to support incarcerated businesses.

Orders available at: billiondollarblueprintmerch.com

www.ingramcontent.com/pod-product-compliance
Lightning Source LLC
Chambersburg PA
CBHW060542130626
46553CB00002B/860